Bringing the Standards for Foreign Language Learning to Life

Deborah Blaz

EYE ON EDUCATION

6 DEPOT WAY WEST, SUITE 106

LARCHMONT, NY 10538

(914) 833–0551

(914) 833–0761 fax

www.eyeoneducation.com

Library of Congress Cataloging-in-Publication Data

Blaz, Deborah.
　　Bringing the standards for foreign language learning to life / Deborah Blaz.
　　　　p.　cm.
　　Includes bibliographical references.
　　ISBN 1–930556–44–6
　　　1. Language and languages—Study and teaching—United States. 2. National Standards in Foreign Language Education Project (U.S.) I. Title.

　　P57.U5 B58 2002
　　418'.0071'073—dc21

2002072100

10 9 8 7 6 5 4 3 2

Editorial and production services provided by
Richard H. Adin Freelance Editorial Services
52 Oakwood Blvd., Poughkeepsie, NY 12603-4112
(845-471-3566)

Also Available from EYE ON EDUCATION

A Collection of Performance Tasks and Rubrics:
Foreign Languages
by Deborah Blaz

Foreign Language Teacher's Guide to Active Learning
by Deborah Blaz

Teaching Foreign Languages in the Block
by Deborah Blaz

Differentiated Instruction:
A Guide for Middle and High School Teachers
by Amy Benjamin

Better Instruction Through Assessment:
What Your Students Are Trying to Tell You
by Leslie Walker Wilson

Performance Standards and Authentic Learning
by Allan A. Glatthorn

Performance Assessment and Standards-
Based Curricula: The Achievement Cycle
by Allan Glatthorn
with Don Bragaw, Karen Dawkins, and John Parker

Constructivist Strategies: Meeting Standards
and Engaging Adolescent Minds
by Foote, Vermette, and Battaglia

Collaborative Learning in Middle and High School:
Applications and Assessments
by Dawn M. Snodgrass and Mary M. Bevevino

About the Author

Deborah Blaz, a French teacher at Angola High School in Angola, Indiana, is a native of St. Charles, Illinois. She received her B.A. in French and German from Illinois State University, a *diplôme* from the Université de Grenoble in Grenoble, France, and, in 1974, an M.A. in French from the University of Kentucky. Ms. Blaz has taught French and English to grades 7 through 12 for the past 22 years in Indiana. She also serves as foreign language department chair at her school, and teaches adult English classes as a volunteer.

Ms. Blaz is the author of three best-selling reference books, *The Foreign Language Teacher's Guide to Active Learning, Teaching Foreign Languages in the Block,* and *A Collection of Performance Tasks and Rubrics: Foreign Languages.* She has frequently presented on successful teaching strategies at state and national conferences, universities, and high schools. A recipient of the Project E Excellence in Education award in 2000, she was also named Indiana's French Teacher of the Year by the Indiana chapter of the American Association of Teachers of French (IAATF) in 1996, and was named to the All-USA Teacher Team, Honorable Mention, by *USA Today* in 1996.

She may be contacted at Angola High School, 755 S 100 E, Angola, IN 46703.

Acknowledgments

I would like to thank everyone whose advice, encouragement and support has helped me in this endeavor, including Carol Ross Stacy of Newman Smith High School in Carrollton, Texas, who generously allowed me to include her lesson on the perils and pitfalls of Internet translators in Chapter 5. Thanks also to Judith Curiel and her colleagues and to the members of my own Angola High School department—Cynthia Jones, Darlene Lankenau, and Marilyn Myers—who helped me pilot the text evaluation instrument in Chapter 7.

I'd also especially like to express my gratitude to my husband, children, parents, and other family members, as well as to Paul Hoekstra and Dorothy Carregal who reviewed this book in manuscript form, and to my publisher Bob Sickles.

Table of Contents

1

The ACTFL Standards: A Discussion

When I received my copy of the *Standards for Foreign Language Learning in the 21st Century*, I was in awe of the amount of planning, discussion, writing, and rewriting it must have taken to compile this document. Then I was stunned by the seemingly difficult task of aligning my curriculum and daily lessons with it.

I had been operating, as many of us do, on my own little "desert island," lonely but determined to do my best, able to determine my own daily direction but cut off from colleagues and input as to what should be taught and how. And here was contact with the "world" again, but the demands and size of this new input were overwhelming. The *Standards* were, to me, uncharted, uncomfortable territory.

This book is about my attempt to make the *Standards* usable on a daily basis; intelligible to administrators, students, and parents; and shareable with other foreign language teachers.

The National Standards

The national standards for foreign language education center around five goals: Communication, Cultures, Connections, Comparisons, and Communities—the five Cs of foreign language education.

In the 1993 legislation *Goals 2000: Educate America Act,* one of the focuses was on the need for national standards. The discipline of foreign languages was named a core curricular area together with English, mathematics, science, civics and government, economics, arts, history, and geography. However, it was the final subject area to receive the funding to develop national standards.

At that time, in my opinion, most teaching in FL classrooms concentrated on the how (grammar) to say what (vocabulary), with a little bit of culture thrown in. An eleven- member group organized by the American Council for the Teaching of Foreign Languages (ACTFL) began work on defining whether this was enough; what should students know and be able to do?

Not only this original group of educators produced the final document. They were joined by business leaders, government officials, and community members. Drafts of the document were sent to many language teachers (and others) for feedback. After an enormous amount of work and thought, writing and rewriting, the *Standards* were finalized. The resultant organizing principle for foreign language study is communication, which keeps the *how* and the *what*, but also highlights the *why, who,* and the *when.* They seem to have decided that, whereas grammar and vocabulary are essential tools, it is the acquisition of the ability to communicate in meaningful and appropriate ways with users of other languages that is the goal in today's classroom.

Having these national standards is also a way to reassure parents that this is truly an academic curriculum and that the teacher who implements these standards is meeting the levels of required knowledge. Though creativity and innovation are a major part of successful language teaching, those alone will not ensure that a student has what is needed to use the language effectively in a career, for example.

What I like about the standards is that they are expressed in terms of goals regarding behaviors—the five Cs—instead of specific topics. They do not say that an equal amount of time or effort or "credit/points" should be spent on each of the goals; nor do they say how the goals should be met. The details were intentionally omitted so the curricular decisions could be made closer to the classroom, and taking into account things such as the needs of local businesses, a large (or nonexistent) population of native speakers, and so on.

In the 1999 edition, language-specific standards are included for the following languages: Chinese, Classical languages, French, German, Italian, Japanese, Portuguese, Russian and Spanish.

Figure 1.1, which is reprinted with permission from the National Standards in Foreign Language Education Collaborative Project of the ACTFL, shows the basic standards.

Figure 1.1. Standards for Foreign Language Learning

Statement of Philosophy

Language and communication are at the heart of the human experience. The United States must educate students who are linguistically and culturally equipped to communicate successfully in a pluralistic American society and abroad. This imperative envisions a future in which ALL students will develop and maintain proficiency in English and at least one other language, modern or classical. Children who come to school from non-English backgrounds should also have opportunities to develop further proficiencies in their first language.

♦ Communication: Communicate in Languages Other Than English

- **Standard 1.1:** Students engage in conversations, provide and obtain information, express feelings and emotions, and exchange opinions.

- **Standard 1.2:** Students understand and interpret written and spoken language on a variety of topics.

- **Standard 1.3:** Students present information, concepts, and ideas to an audience of listeners or readers on a variety of topics.

♦ Cultures: Gain Knowledge and Understanding of Other Cultures

- **Standard 2.1:** Students demonstrate an understanding of the relationship between the practices and perspectives of the culture studied.

- **Standard 2.2:** Students demonstrate an understanding of the relationship between the products and perspectives of the culture studied.

♦ Connections: Connect with Other Disciplines and Acquire Information

- **Standard 3.1:** Students reinforce and further their knowledge of other disciplines through the foreign language .

- **Standard 3.2:** Students acquire information and recognize the distinctive viewpoints that are only available through the foreign language and its cultures.

♦ Comparisons: Develop Insight into the Nature of Language and Culture

- **Standard 4.1:** Students demonstrate understanding of the nature of language through comparisons of the language studied and their own.

- **Standard 4.2:** Students demonstrate understanding of the concept of culture through comparisons of the cultures studied and their own.

♦ Communities: Participate in Multilingual Communities at Home and Around the World

- **Standard 5.1:** Students use the language both within and beyond the school setting.

- **Standard 5.2:** Students show evidence of becoming life-long learners by using the language for personal enjoyment and enrichment.

Basic Truths About the Standards

My initial impression of the *Standards* was that, because there were five Cs, all five needed to be covered to an equal extent. This troubled me a bit, as I felt that two of the Cs, Communication and Culture, had been almost exclusively what I did in my classroom. However, over the next year or so as I began to intentionally implement them, I realized several basic truths about the *Standards*:

- The five strands under which the standards are organized—Communication, Culture, Connections, Comparisons and Communities —are meant to be interwoven among themselves, with as many as possible in each unit taught. However, certain units will more easily lend themselves to a particular C (or two) than to all five.

- Just because there are five Cs doesn't mean every unit has to contain all five. Don't stress too much if a unit is weak in several standards.

- It is possible to cover each C as a separate entity if desired.

- Meeting each standard will contribute to reaching the other standards. (They often overlap.)

- Just make sure you do all five at least once each level. Look at things from a yearly or multiyearly perspective. Ask yourself: is a single high-quality unit on one standard sufficient? (The old *quality vs. quantity* issue that we must all grapple with.)

- Most texts still address primarily the first two Cs, though some effort has been made by publishers since 2000 to include a bit of the others. Having just been through textbook adoption, it is still obvious to me that we will still have to supplement a lot to cover all five. This book contains a chapter for each C, with suggestions and ideas.

- There is another reason the *Standards* are a bit vague. Some activities that are easy to do for one language (for example, study all the countries that speak your language, for French, Arabic, or Spanish) would be unfeasible for others (for example, American Sign Language, Hebrew, Italian, or Latin). So there is a lot of "wiggle room" which is also great for creative teachers.

- The national standards correlate nicely with other educational perspectives. For an example, in Figure 1.2, you will find a list of the standards along with at least one of Gardner's eight intelligences that nicely fits that standard. So, if you have units planned around attempts to appeal to each intelligence, you may be able to easily correlate those units with the *Standards* by using this chart!

Figure 1.2. Standards That Appeal to Multiple Intelligences

	Intelligence	*Explanation*
• **Standard 1:** Communication: Communicate in Languages Other Than English	• Linguistic Intelligence • Interpersonal	• Listening, speaking, reading and writing • Communicating and collaborating with others
• **Standard 2:** Cultures: Gain Knowledge and Understanding of Other Cultures	• Logical-Mathematical • Visual-Spatial Kinesthetic • Musical	• Deduction, induction, (cultural patterns), perceiving imagery (art) • Bodily movements and manipulating objects (dance and cooking) • Rhythm, tone, melody and pitch (music/singing)
• **Standard 3:** Connections: Connect with Other Disciplines and Acquire Information	• Naturalist • Interpersonal	• Making connections with elements in nature • Collaborating and sharing information
• **Standard 4:** Comparisons: Develop Insight into the Nature of Language and Culture	• Logical-Mathematical	• Perceiving patterns (comparing target language and culture with native language and culture)
• **Standard 5:** Communities: Participate in Multilingual Communities at Home and Around the World	• Interpersonal • Intrapersonal	• Communicating and collaborating with others • Using the language for personal enjoyment and enrichment

♦ Complying with the national standards is voluntary. Some states (New York and Arizona, for instance) already had their own standards and are keeping them. However, many states are now writing and adopting curriculum based upon the National Standards. Try to find out what's happening in your state, and see if you can give input before the decision is taken out of your hands.

Thinking About Implementation: A Story

One of my favorite stories (paraphrased from Steven R. Covey, *The 7 Habits of Highly Effective People*) is about a speaker giving a demonstration to a group of students. Standing near a cabinet, he brought out a large jar, and then a bag of fist-sized rocks. He carefully placed each rock in the jar, filling it to the top, and asked, "Is the jar full?"

The class nodded, and he sighed, "No," and took out a bag of gravel. This he poured over the rocks, shaking the jar until it had sifted through into all the spaces between the rocks, and again he asked, "Is it full?"

One student suggested, "Maybe not?" and the speaker nodded approvingly, pulling out a bag of sand, and repeating what he'd done with the gravel. And again, he asked the students, "Is it full?"

"No!" they shouted, and he beamed at them and brought out a pitcher of water, pouring it into the jar until it overflowed.

"Now," continued the speaker, "what was the point of this demonstration?"

"Oh," said the same student who spoke earlier in the story. "That's easy. No matter what, you can always find space for a few more things."

"Oh, no" disagreed the speaker. "It's that if you don't put in the big rocks first, they won't all fit."

Implementing the Standards in Your Classroom

Keeping the above story firmly in mind, consider each course/level you teach and determine the key concepts a student must have by the end of his or her term in your classroom.

Step 1: Set Goals

Every time I write curriculum, and every day I write a lesson plan, I think: What is my "big rock" for today? What "big rocks" are in this chapter, this unit? What "big rocks" must I cover for this level?

Your first step in implementing the five Cs is to list your big rocks (usually, units or concepts) for each level, each on a separate piece of paper (see Figure 1.3).

Figure 1.3. Evaluation Form

BIG ROCK:

Activities	Communication			Culture		Connections		Comparisons		Communities		Resources
	1.1	1.2	1.3	2.1	2.2	3.1	3.2	4.1	4.2	5.1	5.2	
List below:	Interpersonal	Interpretive	Presentational	Practices	Products	Intercurricular	Viewpoints	Language	Culture	Use within & out	Enjoy/enrich	List below:
1												
2												
3												
4												
5												
6												
7												
8												
9												
10												

Step 2: Plan Activities

Next, list the activities students will do to learn that "rock." Then, using the grid, check the Cs that apply to each activity.

Step 3: Complement or Supplement to Include More Standards

If you're like me, most of the activities will be parts of either Standard 1 or 2. Don't worry. That's normal. Realize some units apply better to some standards than others.

Look at Step 1, and see if any of the other Cs can be added to the "rock"—can you modify an activity to make it a 3, 4, or a 5? Can you complement or supplement what you already do to include at least one more standard? (See Figure 1.4 for suggestions, or the appropriate chapter later in this text.)

Step 4: List Available Resources

Now that you've decided on your "big rocks" and activities, consider the sources available:

- ♦ Textbook. For some teachers, a text chapter is only a small part of a unit. For others, each chapter is an instructional unit. If you decide on a thematic approach, or write your own TPRS materials, you may not use a text at all. (See Chapter 6 on evaluating a text.)

- ♦ Ancillary materials with text. Many texts come with conversation cards, overhead transparencies, partner worksheets, audio and video tapes, CD-ROMs, and/or online resources.

- ♦ Supplementary materials you've purchased. We all have loads of manipulatives, realia (coins, musical instruments, clothing, and many other items), as well as photos, slides, books, magazines, art, videos, music, posters, and so on.

- ♦ Curriculum. Hopefully, you were able to take part in writing it.

- ♦ Technology available. How many computers do you have access to, and how often? Is the Internet accessible? E-mail? Audio and video possibilities? What software do you have available or can you purchase? Do you have a digital camera or video camera?

- ♦ Student profile. Students' economic levels, family background, and career aspirations will greatly influence your students' needs and interests, so this is an important item to keep in mind as you decide on your activities.

Figure 1.4. Suggested Methods of Adding Cs

Connections	Add numbers (Math "connection"): ♦ Surveys, reporting percentages ♦ Giving typical prices and converting those to dollars Add art or music (Fine Arts): ♦ Teach vocabulary using famous paintings ♦ Use songs, especially those with movements
Comparisons	Use realia: ♦ Bring in magazines, newspapers, or artifacts ♦ Go online to look at information at its source Plan an interdisciplinary unit with another teacher, perhaps even schoolwide (for example, themes like Celebrations, Our World/ecology, Love).
Communities	Add a "service component": ♦ Have students bring in items (food/clothing) to donate to needy ♦ Make art/craft projects and give them to area groups. (Nursing homes and/or shut-ins can be found in the U.S. or abroad.) ♦ Perform for others: sing/dance/read aloud Add a "current events" with a service component: ♦ Raise consciousnesses by raising money or donations for disaster relief after volcanic eruptions, hurricanes, famine, earthquakes, bombings, etc. Some resources for this will be found in Chapter 6. ♦ Start a chapter of Amnesty International (Nobel Prize for Peace 1999) and write Urgent Action letters on behalf of prisoners of conscience —may often be done in the target language. This organization is very active at many college campuses, and can be continued for life.

♦ Community resources. Ask yourself if there are any native speakers, local businesses or service organizations, universities, museums, restaurants, theaters, or other places where you could take students, find guest speakers, have students perform, and so on.

♦ Colleagues as resources. Try to get together often with teachers who either teach your subject area and have a similar wish to implement all five standards, or find colleagues in related fields. (Fine arts, English, and social studies are easy tie-ins for a foreign language teacher, and a media center specialist/librarian can be a font of information on the technology and print resources available.) Brainstorm. Run your ideas past them for comments before you try them on the students. Share successes and let them cheer you up when something didn't go as well as planned. Collaboration is very important!

List all the above resources available for each activity you've listed in Steps 2 and 3.

Step 5: Evaluate and Prune

Take into consideration how full the curriculum already is, how important the standards are, and how these competing priorities can be reconciled. You'll undoubtedly need to discard some exercises and activities, retaining those most critical Big Rocks for student attainment of curriculum, chapter objectives, and national standards.

I like using this chart because it shows me very easily those areas that I am ignoring or addressing inadequately. This might be a good exercise to do for those who think they either don't "get" the *Standards* or are afraid they're not doing them "right," or those who need to document that they are doing these, for parents or administrators.

I predict you'll be pleasantly surprised in many cases by all you *do* do that supports the *Standards*.

Figure 1.5 (pp. 11–13) is an example of a unit on health, plugged into the grid and adjusted in an attempt to include all five Cs.

Communication is the Cornerstone

Notice that many activities use Communication as well as another standard. As I stated previously, I think that for most of us the communication standard is the core of what we do. It is also an essential part of anything leading to the goals of the other standards.

So real communicative activities will naturally tend to address multiple goals, and using the standards chart will make you very aware of this.

Using the standards, I think of myself as a puppeteer pulling on strings. Some strings, though they work, aren't as necessary as others, and so I use them less. And so I keep my focus on Communication, and the rest of the standards fall easily into place around it.

(Text continues on page 14.)

Figure 1.5. Evaluation Form

BIG ROCK: Students will be able to discuss their health and what they do to remain in good health.

Activities	Communication			Culture		Connections		Comparisons		Communities		Resources
	1.1	1.2	1.3	2.1	2.2	3.1	3.2	4.1	4.2	5.1	5.2	
	Converse	Read/Write	Present Info	Practices	Products	Intercurricular	Viewpoints	Language	Culture	Use within & out	Enjoy enrich	
List below:												List below:
1 Describe activities people do to be physically fit, in USA and in target culture	X		X	X						X	X	Story in text / Class discussion / Interview native speakers
2 Read news ads in target language		X			X							Workbook / Newspapers / Online article
3 Identify differences between their practices & ours				X		X (P.E.)	X		X			Sports page / Text illustrations / Native speaker / Venn diagram

(*Figure continues on next page.*)

Activities	Communication			Culture		Connections		Comparisons		Communities		Resources
	1.1 Converse	1.2 Read/Write	1.3 Present Info	2.1 Practices	2.2 Products	3.1 Intercurricular	3.2 Viewpoints	4.1 Language	4.2 Culture	5.1 Use within & out	5.2 Enjoy enrich	
List below:												List below:
4 Look at a culturally-based food pyramid	X	X		X		X FACS			X		X	Online or local farm bureau extension
5 VOCAB: body parts sports exercises commands diseases remedies	X	X	X	X		X Fine Arts						Text Grocery store field trip Posters Print & online materials Songs
Look for cognates								X				Discussion

| Activities | Communication | | | Culture | | Connections | | Comparisons | | Communities | | Resources |
	1.1 Converse	1.2 Read/Write	1.3 Present Info	2.1 Practices	2.2 Products	3.1 Intercurricular	3.2 Viewpoints	4.1 Language	4.2 Culture	5.1 Use within & out	5.2 Enjoy enrich	List below:
List below:												Interdisciplinary with health teacher, journalism teacher and/or FACS teacher
6 Survey on sports & health practices:												
develop	X	X				X						
conduct on selves	X	X				X						
compile results,	X	X				X						
give to keypals via e-mail,		X				X Math						
write article on results		X	X								X	
7 Skit on visit to nurse: write, perform for upper level classes	X	X	X								X	School nurse Local hospitals or clinics Sample skit in text Video of hospital visit

Note: FACS: Family and Consumer Science, formerly called Home Economics

Involve the Students in Implementation

Let's remember that kids come into our classroom with certain needs and wants when it comes to deciding what to learn, how much to learn, and so on. Why not let them know what the national standards are, and let their interests guide you in planning portions of the unit?

To teach the national standards, on the very first day of class, I like to show students an overhead page or a PowerPoint presentation on the "Five Cs of Foreign Language Learning." Then they break up into five groups, and each is assigned one of the five Cs. Each group then makes a collage poster about their "C word" and how it relates to learning French. (Of course, you'd adapt this for your own target language.) I walk around as they work, giving them suggestions of units they'll be doing this year. The posters are then prominently displayed in the classroom (or in the hallway) for a couple weeks, giving them a taste of what's to come as well as reminders why French (or any language) is really useful outside the classroom. There are a lot fewer questions from them now, too, along the lines of "How come we gotta do this?"

The ways they choose to illustrate their "C word" will also give you an idea of what they view as interesting or important in what you've told them will be covered at that level, a valuable insight for you as to what motivates your students. Knowledge of students' goals/wants/needs is critical; one of my favorite slogans to keep in mind when writing lesson plans is:

> When fishing, what do you put on the hook: what you like, or what the fish likes?

A Few Final Comments

Because I make an effort to survey my students each year to determine their learning styles, I have noticed that the National Standards correlate nicely with Gardner's intelligences (Figure 1.2, p. 5). Most teachers will agree that using variety is the best way to help students learn better; and trying to address multiple intelligences, brain research, or the National Standards are all going to encourage us to try a larger variety of teaching strategies.

Addressing the National Standards has also freed me from feeling an obligation to cover everything in the book in the order it is presented. As an example, take a typical food unit. Most of my kids were never going to order cabbage or snails, and had never seen an artichoke. Now I teach the foods that will be found in a typical menu or recipe, and make sure every student can describe his/her favorite sandwich ingredients, favorite ice cream flavor and favorite meal, as well as knowing words for foods they absolutely despise, so they don't accidentally order those. Along with the food vocabulary, we learn quantities (a pound of, a slice of, a bottle of), commands (Bring me … Give me …), and also comparatives (too salty, more sugar, less mustard), which are in other areas of the book. The book barely touches upon typical cuisine, so we go to recipes in books and on the Internet as well as to restaurants to bring in the cultural component (as well as, hopefully, the lifelong enrichment and enjoyment aspect). Try to be as realistic as possible. It's not hard, the kids like it better, so they speak better, are more motivated, and remember more.

An Example

Instead of the usual dry study of Picasso (students read his biography, teacher presents and explains his *Guernica* and tries to elicit student discussion), why not connect it to kids' learning styles and contemporary events? After doing a brief biographical lesson, take copies of several of his works and cut them into squares. Partner two students, with one getting one of the cut-up picture and the other a complete copy of it. Partner A will then explain to Partner B how to correctly assemble the painting, without showing him/her the complete copy until they are finished. Then, post the complete copies for all the students to see, and have students decide what the main characteristics of his work are, and then make a portrait of their partner, Picasso-style. Follow the presentation of these masterpieces with a discussion of Perspectives/Perceptions that can lead to connections between *Guernica* and current events such as bombings or school shootings. Use your imagination and see how much your students retain, and if you lack imagination, check the archives of or join the FL-TEACH listserv, an Internet group of thousands of extremely creative foreign language teachers who will be happy to share ideas with you. The Internet address is: http://listserv.buffalo.edu/archives/flteach.html.

For most of us the standards are a document that validates the sorts of things that we are already doing in our classroom and a reminder not to forget certain aspects. One final metaphor for using these standards: as a teacher using the national standards, you don't need to invent a new recipe, but just rethink what you've already done, evaluating, analyzing, synthesizing, and then reroll the dough and try a new cookie cutter!

2
Standard 1: Communication

> ♦ Communicate in Languages Other Than English
>
> • Standard 1.1: Students engage in conversations, provide and obtain information, express feelings and emotions, and exchange opinions.
>
> • Standard 1.2: Students understand and interpret written and spoken language on a variety of topics.
>
> • Standard 1.3: Students present information, concepts, and ideas to an audience of listeners or readers on a variety of topics.

Communication is the heart of second language study, whether the communication takes place face-to-face, in writing, or across centuries through the reading of literature. What opportunities are there in your classroom for students to participate in face-to-face interaction, originate or interpret written and spoken messages, and communicate meaningfully in written or spoken form?

Important Factors to Consider

Comprehensible, Interesting, Relevant, and Motivating

When doing communicative activities in the classroom, four important aspects of communication that, in my opinion, are often neglected or ignored, must be considered. The first is that both the information and the activities must, in addition to being comprehensible, be *interesting, relevant, and motivating*. The best way to do this is to make sure that students have as much contact as possible with authentic speech, texts, newscasts, and other visual materials. Even beginning level students, after being pretaught key words and phrases and given specific things to look for, can handle watching or listening to unedited authentic materials in the target language. If they know the materials are authentic, and if the materials are interesting to them (such as music videos, movies, game shows, comic books, and other items students their age enjoy), they will certainly be motivated and enthusiastic. Enthusiasm is a major factor influencing success in foreign language study.

Another way to create a perception of relevancy is to do frequent simulations. My students are given passports on the first day of school, and in succeeding days we simulate taking public transportation, checking into a hotel, buying train tickets, and other daily activities of a person who speaks the target language.

A third method that is viewed as authentic by students is to teach them things they already know in their own language, but in the target language. Students love to recite nursery rhymes, the Lord's Prayer, or the Pledge of Allegiance in a new language, just as they like to see movies they already know, such as Disney favorites, in the target language, and to learn familiar songs.

Increase Students' Comfort Levels

A second important thing to keep in mind is that students should not be asked or forced to participate on a more personal level than they feel comfortable with. Try to provide opportunities for students to find a nonthreatening topic or a nonthreatening method of participation.

For example, I have a classroom collection of stuffed animals. Students, when speaking for the animal, will often speak more, and more willingly, than if asked to speak as themselves. The animals can also have more "colorful" lives than the students, and thereby use more vocabulary. (For example, eating preferences for a squirrel or another herbivore make students who don't willingly eat many vegetables practice that vocabulary.)

Some teachers have students make puppets out of paper lunch bags. By not fully unfolding the top, but leaving it as a sort of flap, you can draw a top and bottom half of the mouth and have a puppet whose mouth opens and closes, and which can easily be folded flat and stored in a folder or book. Sock puppets or glove puppets (like Señor Wences on the old Ed Sullivan show) are also inexpensive. I recently saw Martha Stewart demonstrate some cute puppets made from old tennis balls: have someone cut a slash in the ball first to serve as a mouth, and then use felt, yarn, markers, and whatever else is available to make a hand puppet.

Another way to make speaking nonthreatening is to role-play. In my intermediate- and advanced-level classes, I have students create an alter ego, with another name, job, personality, goals, and even style of dress. On appointed days, they come to class "in character" and plan a trip, have a party (and spread rumors about each other), visit the sick in a hospital, find a treasure map and follow it, or whatever fits well with the plot I have devised. We do a murder mystery, an action adventure, or a soap opera. Because the students are not supposed to play themselves, they don't judge what each other wears, says, or does as harshly as if they were required to give an honest performance.

Place Students in Small Groups

A third way to stimulate student participation is to have most such experiences take place in small group settings. Using strategies such as Inside-Outside circle (which has various other names), partners, Think-Pair-Square (a student and partner who've already discussed the topic get together with another pair of students) and other similar activities allow students to talk without twenty or more pair of eyes on them, and without that stress, communication flows more freely.

Use Variety

Finally, the third important factor is to provide a variety of topics or exercises for them to choose from. In this way, students can choose one that they are comfortable with and know a fair amount about.

For example, instead of "Tell about the last picnic you were on" (taken directly from the text I currently am using), you might ask a student to describe a memory that is happy, or sad, or exciting. Other choices might be

+ unusual
+ frightening
+ embarrassing
+ fantastic
+ dreamlike
+ annoying
+ funny

You could ask students to "impress us by displaying your knowledge." Students could choose from the following list:

+ a hobby
+ something you've learned in another class
+ instructions on how to do something
+ a thing you've written, made or created
+ something you've experienced

- ◆ something you've invented
- ◆ ?? (see teacher for approval)

Keep the four considerations described here in mind when devising a communication activity, and it will be much more successful.

Looking at Standard 1 in Depth

The three divisions of this standard can, I think, be paraphrased into the three modes of communication often listed in books: Standard 1.1 as interpersonal communication, Standards 1.2 as interpretive communication, and Standard 1.3 as presentational communication. Let's look at each one separately.

For each, I will define the standard and list activities that fulfill that standard that most teachers routinely use in their classrooms. Then I will give some more unusual lessons or projects that would be appropriate for that standard. Because this book is intended for teachers of all languages, I generally put the handouts and instructions in English, whereas in the classroom, they would be in the target language, of course.

Finally, because communications activities are so proficiency-based, I have divided each substandard into Beginner-, Intermediate-, and Advanced-level activities. Coincidentally, this arrangement makes this chapter better adapted to the New York standards and those of other states that were written before the national standards were established, as well as with college classes. Beginner level, for example, would contain the easier activities, best suited to early elementary or first-year secondary. I leave it up to the individual teacher to determine what level of activity a particular group of students needs. I've had second-year students who are still only capable of basic interactions, and other groups at the same level who want the challenge of something more difficult.

Standard 1.1: Interpersonal Communication

Students engage in conversations, provide and obtain information, express feelings and emotions, and exchange opinions.

This standard focuses on interpersonal communication, that is, direct oral or written communication between individuals who are in personal contact. This standard refers to students' ability to converse in a culturally appropriate manner. Figure 2.1 lists some of the many activities teachers commonly use to stimulate or simulate conversation in their classrooms.

Figure 2.1. Interpersonal Communication Activities

bingo/vocabulary bingo	joke	riddle
board race	journal	roleplay
conversation	logical continuation of story	selective listening
debate	mock interview	seminar
dialogue	music	simulation
discussion	note-taking	skit
dramatic reading	paraphrase/restate	Socratic seminar
explanation	pair worksheets (each has only half the information)	TPR (Total Physical Response)
flyswatter	peer tutorial	TPRS (TPR Storytelling)
inside-outside circle	question-and-answer	
interview	rebus stories	

The best activities for this are simple ones with a real-life application, such as

♦ planning a trip, menu or party

♦ doing a survey

♦ comparing experiences, likes or dislikes

♦ describing a person or event that is meaningful (including using circumlocution)

In other words, have them do something that they'll enjoy and which will get them talking right away.

Beginner-Level Activities

Beginners can be expected to ask or give short answers to questions in person, on the telephone (or voice mail), using audio or videotapes, or by writing letters or using e-mail. Typical topics for this level are social situations such as greeting or leave-taking, introducing someone, thanking someone, apologizing for something; or descriptions of family or nonfamily members, favorite items including foods, and/or events at home or at school including holidays.

They might also be expected to give or respond to simple commands. For example they can be asked to move around the room, perform basic actions such as rolling or throwing a ball, or participate in games such as Simon Says. A favorite game of my summer school students for learning new vocabulary is Pass It.

Pass It

1. Have students sit in a circle. Give each an item. This can be a plastic piece of food, a flashcard with a picture, a hygiene item like soap or toothpaste—whatever vocabulary is in the current unit.

2. First, have everyone in the class go around and name all the items in the circle. I usually say them first, and have students repeat them. We discuss them as we do this, too: is it red? green? big? small? and so on. I may also tell them to put in on their head, or other TPR suggestions we've been working on.

3. Then I name the items at random, and the student with that item displays it.

4. Next, we pass the items while I play some music in the target language. When I stop the music, everyone stops passing the objects, and I ask, "Who has the (object)?" and the student with the object named shouts out the word in the target language.

5. We repeat passing the items until students seem comfortable with the new vocabulary.

Here is another good beginner-level interpersonal communication activity:

"What a Mess!" Slumber Party

Level: Beginner (including elementary)

Materials needed: stuffed animals (students' own or chosen from a classroom collection)

1. Have students choose and name and make a name tag for their animal. Have them introduce their animal to as many other animals in the room as possible. Incorporate other vocabulary by having the animal also state its nationality or favorite color, favorite food, or whatever you would like.

2. Tell the kids that their animal will be sleeping overnight in the classroom at the end of the day. Have them bed down their animal, and either have the student read or tell their animal a bedtime story, or you as teacher read everyone a bedtime story.

3. Just before the end of the class (or day), have students wish their animal good night and tell them to behave themselves. Then you leave with the students, noisily locking the door behind you all.

4. In the morning before students arrive, or whenever you will be unobserved, go back into the classroom and mess it up. Knock over

something, put a poster upside down, move animals together, open a window or drawer, scribble on the board—everything you can think of. Then lock the door and leave.

5. Arrive at the same time the students do. Walk in with the students. Have them join you in expressing amazement/shock/anger at the mess inside. Scold your animal (and have the kids copy what you say).

6. Have the students figure out what's different in the room, and who did it. List these on the board.

7. Have students and animals help you clean up the mess. Have the animals apologize.

8. Turn this into a short composition; it's really good practice for the past tense, and a lot of the vocabulary is already on the board.

Preposition Race

1. Get two cardboard boxes, and divide the class into two teams.

2. Enlist a student from each teamand have them each stand beside a box.

3. Have a different student for each preposition. Alternating teams, shout prepositions to the volunteers, who must jump in, out, beside, around, far from, close to, over, on, or between the two boxes. Prepositions may not be repeated during a round, so students must listen to what has already been called out.

4. Give a point to the side whose volunteer understands the preposition and positions himself correctly, first.

Intermediate-Level Activities

Students at this level will

♦ exchange information at greater length, providing more information than asked for. For example, if asked, "Are you from Chicago?" they might say, "No, but I visited there last summer. My cousin lives there." or "Yes, but I was born in Michigan."

♦ be capable of circumlocution activities. Circumlocution involves explaining what something is without using the word for it, sort of like the old game show Password. This is a useful skill for explaining uniquely American cultural concepts such as cheerleading, common objects ("How would you describe a "teeter totter" to an exchange student so he would know what you were talking about?"), or foods such as Jell-O or brownies, or finally, coping strategies for when one doesn't yet know the word (or has forgotten the word) in the target language.

♦ begin expressing feelings and explaining why they feel that way. For example, I have my students play the Ungame (a board game purchased at a garage sale). In this they draw a card that asks them to tell something that makes them sad or scared or happy or proud, what they'd say to someone in a certain situation, and so on. If they can do this, they move their marker a certain number of spaces on a board. Something like this could easily be made over summer vacation; involve colleagues or friends to help you think of situations.

Here are several good intermediate interpersonal communications activities:

Simple Phone Call

Level: Intermediate

Needs: access to a telephone. May require the presence of an adult (see instructions).

1. Give students a topic for a telephone conversation. Brainstorm any vocabulary that might be necessary for a conversation on that topic, and review how to answer a telephone and other telephone phrases such as "Just a minute."

A typical assignment for a telephone message left on an answering machine might be like this:

> Greet the person who answers and identify yourself.
>
> Tell two things you did to help out around the house this week.
>
> Ask a question.
>
> Say goodbye.

A typical assignment for a conversation at this level might be:

> Greet the person who answers and identify yourself.
>
> Invite them to do something with you at a specific place and time.
>
> They refuse, because they are busy/don't want to.
>
> They suggest a different activity.
>
> Agree to do that.
>
> Agree on a time and place to meet.
>
> Say goodbye.

2. Have students either call your voice mail at school, your answering machine at home and leave a message, or call a partner and have a conversation (and tape the conversation on speakerphone, or have a parent or guardian verify that the conversation took place). Of course, I make allowances for students without a telephone, or who are deaf, usually by having a face-to-face conversation on a similar topic.

3. Either during or immediately after the call, have students fill out a form with information.

    For a phone message, I play back the messages for my students, and have them fill out a form such as the one in Figure 2.2.

Figure 2.2. Phone Message Record Form

Name

	The two things I said I did:	And who else said the same ones:
1.	_____	_____
2.	_____	_____
	Two things I didn't do:	And who did them:
1.	_____	_____
2.	_____	_____

Words I heard classmates mispronounce: (there hopefully won't be any!)

Other errors I heard: _____

For telephone conversations, I have students fill out a form such as the one in Figure 2.3.

Figure 2.3. Telephone Conversation Record Form

Name _____   Person called _____

The first thing your partner said: _____

What you invited him/her to do with you: _____

What they suggested instead: _____

Time and place you decided to meet: _____

Ordinary/Extraordinary

Ask students to help brainstorm *different and unusual* things related to the topic in the current chapter, things such as

- times or places to brush one's teeth
- places to study
- things to do for a headache
- sandwich fillings
- flavors of ice cream
- people they'd like to be President
- school colors or mascots

Give a prize to your favorite suggestion, or to the last new suggestion made (this stimulates more effort and more participation).

Never-Never Land

Requirements: knowledge of preterit/passé composé tense. A high-interest activity!

1. Introduce the word/structure necessary to say "never." Assign at least five sentences about things students have never done before.

2. Give each student about ten poker chips, tickets, dried lima beans, or some sort of marker. (I like ones that make a noise as they drop it in a container.) Take turns saying a "never" sentence and then passing the container; every student who HAS done that thing must put in one of his/her markers.

3. Continue until there are only two students with any markers left. Reward the first one out ("most experienced") and the last ones ("most inexperienced").

When I Was a Child...

Here are interview questions I have students use to interview each other when we study the imperfect tense; many are adaptable to present tense interviews.

When you were a child, what, or who, was your favorite

1. Play activity?

2. Toy?

3. Friend?

4. Place to go, and why?

5. Food? Candy?

6. Hobby?

7. Comic strip?

8. TV show?

9. Movie/video?

10. Book or story?

11. Song?

12. Outfit?

13. Grownup other than family, and why?

14. Teacher and why?

15. Relative (not parent or guardian) and why?

16. Holiday, and why?

17. Memory of snow?

18. Memory at a beach or pool?

19. Thing to do that was scary?

20. Ride at the amusement park?

21. Future job?

Staged Storytelling

Level: Intermediate:

Goal: practice the use of the imperfect and preterite/passé composé

1. Arrange for a colleague or other staff member who is not busy to come to your room.

2. Arrange to videotape what occurs: set camera up as unobtrusively as possible, with a wide-angle view of the classroom.

3. The colleague should enter the room and, soon begin to behave very strangely. This can involve wearing something odd, shouting something, manipulating objects in the classroom, doing a few dance steps—at least five things. Try to have involve various students: give one a kiss on the cheek, take something of theirs, mess up hair, or whatever this colleague is comfortable doing. They should then exit as dramatically as possible.

4. Students will be somewhat in shock. Tell them you have a videotape and they will view things again. Tell them to write down what happens, and how they felt, with as many details as possible, without talking to each other.

5. Then, assign a partner. Have them take turns relating the events that occurred, helping each other say them in the target language and check for accuracy in use of verb tenses. If needed, give them guidelines on what they should discuss. Obviously what your colleague did will be in the preterit, but most other description—for example feelings, looks and clothes, and other descriptive events like the date and time, what the class was doing before the person entered, and so on—will be in the imperfect.

This can also be turned into a writing assignment. I often use this instead of a standardized test at the end of a unit.

Circumlocution Vocabulary "Password"

1. Introduce phrases useful in target language circumlocution. Typical phrases are shown in Figure 2.4.

Figure 2.4. Phrases for Circumlocution

	French	*German*	*Spanish*
It's a thing that …	C'est une chose que	Es ist eine Dinge/Sache die	Es una cosa que
It's a person who …	C'est une personne qui	Es est eine Person die/wer	Es una persona que
You use it to …	On l'utilise pour	Sie verwenden es, um zu	Tu lo/la utilizas para
You say it when …	Tu le dis quand	Du sagst es wenn	Tu lo/la digas cuando
You need it for …	Il le faut pour	Du brauchst/ Du benötigst es für	Tu lo/la necesitas para
You find it in …	Tu le/la trouves à	Du findest es in/am	Tu lo/la encuentras en

2. Introduce a circumlocution game, using Inside Outside Circle. (Partner students and have them sit facing each other. Then, either have students move to be with a new partner, or pass the cards so that they try them all.) Give half the students a card with a new vocabulary word, and have them circumlocute, with a 47-second time limit. They get a point for every one they get correct. Any use of English results in a 3-point penalty.

Vacation Postcards

This usually follows an activity in which I divide the class into thirds. One group are travel agents, and each student gets a brochure offering two or three different package tours, all with different destinations, prices, methods of transportation, and attractions. For example, one is mostly outdoors with Spartan accommodations, one has a variety of cultural events, another is mostly elegant, expensive things to do, and so on. Students draw cards with their budget (how much they can spend) and goal ("You are looking for somewhere quiet and stress-free") and then they visit the travel agents and find the best tour for them.

I design this so that students will go to all the major cities that speak the target language, plus additional tourist spots such as London, New York, Florida, California, Hawaii and other places my students usually go for spring break. As a follow-up activity, they must write a postcard from the trip.

1. Tell each student to write a postcard from their "vacation" at this spot that includes when they arrived, who they are with, two things they have done, one thing they ate or drank, if they are having fun,

and when they'll be back. Make each item one point, with a point for a correct salutation, another for a culturally appropriate closing, and one for a color illustration for the postcard, and you have a ten-point project.

2. Collect cards, then hand them back for corrections, and then have students pass them around and read them.

Advanced Interpersonal Communication Activities

At this level, students can be expected to give opinions supported by facts. They

- ♦ should be able to (in alphabetical order) advise, agree, argue, complain, convince, debate, direct, negotiate, praise, propose, request, suggest or warn about a variety of issues.

- ♦ narrate extended anecdotes or original stories.

- ♦ use idiomatic expressions appropriately.

Here are some advanced-level activities I've found students like:

To Tell the Truth

1. Have students make a statement, either real or imaginary.

2. The other students in the class must guess if it is true or false, supporting their opinions with reasons for this belief.

Dear Abby/Chère Lucile

Have students, either orally or in writing, share suggestions on how to

- ♦ keep their temper

- ♦ get out of a bad mood

- ♦ get to class on time

- ♦ make someone happy

- ♦ ask their parents for a special privilege

- ♦ say "no" to drugs

- ♦ have a great weekend without spending much money

Conversation Starters

1. Have each student write one sentence on a strip of paper and fold it up.

2. Redistribute the sentences so that no student gets the one he/she has written.

3. Put students in small groups (three or four), and give them five to ten minutes to come up with a short skit that incorporates all three sentences. The scene can be about anything, but it must:

    *   be a fairly realistic conversation

    *   "go somewhere" (plot)

Variations: have each group write sentences to send to another group.

Standard 1.2: Interpretive Communication

Students understand and interpret written and spoken language on a variety of topics.

Without mastering this mode, the worlds of fantasy and inspiration, and the intellectual and esthetic pleasures that literature opens up would be unavailable. This standard ties in very handily with Standard 2 (Culture) as well, because, like the previous interpersonal communication standard, the best materials and format for this standard are those that are as authentic as possible.

Figure 2.5 lists some of the many activities teachers commonly use to stimulate reading and/or listening skills in their classrooms.

Figure 2.5. Interpretive Communication Activities

advice column	graphic organizer	poem
analysis	job application	poster
book jacket or record cover	journal entry	recipe
book report	letter	short story
booklet (family, self, etc.)	newspaper	simile or metaphor
brochure	note or memo	summary
fairy tale	pamphlet	time line

Beginner-Level Activities

Beginners need to grasp the main idea of an oral or written narrative that uses familiar themes such as a well-known fairy tale, common daily routines, and simple vocabulary and sentence construction. Students would be asked to listen to or read authentic signs, billboards, posters, newspaper headlines, labels, programs from concerts, timetables, maps, menus, song lyrics, and instruction sheets. After reading or hearing the selection, they are expected to be able to perform tasks such as those on the following list:

♦ Identify simple words or phrases, written or recorded

♦ Identify a person or an object from an oral or written description

♦ Correctly interpret a gesture or intonation used

♦ List the main ideas and principal characteristics of short stories or children's literature,

♦ Follow simple instructions

Here is an enjoyable beginning level listening activity for students:

How the Days of the Week Got Their Names

(For Chinese or Japanese, use How the Months Got Their Names, with appropriate visuals depicting the race of the twelve animals.)

Level: Beginning

Needs: visuals for each day of the week, for felt board, overhead, or just on cardstock to show the class

Goal: to help students remember the days of the week by tying these words to knowledge already learned in other subject areas (Standard 3: Connections)

1. Review the names for the days of the week with students.

2. Using visuals, explain how each day got its name. Use the chart in Figure 2.6 to find the explanation appropriate to the target language.

3. Put up the pictures in the classroom and have students practice for several days retelling the stories for the days.

Figure 2.6 Chart for How the Days of the Week Got Their Names

Day	Span	Explanation: Roman gods	Fr	Explanation: Roman gods	Ger	Explanation: German gods
Mon.	lunes	Moon Day	lundi	Moon Day	Montag	Moon Day
Tues.	martes	Mars, god of war	mardi	Mars	Dienstag	Tiw/Tiu god of war
Wed.	miercoles	Mercury	mercredi	Mercury	Mittwoch	"midweek"
Thurs.	jueves	Jove/Jupiter, king of gods	jeudi	Jove/Jupiter	Donnerstag	Donner, thunder
Fri.	viernes	Venus, goddess of love	vendredi	Venus	Freitag	Freia, queen of the gods
Sat.	sabadi	Saturn, god of underworld	samedi	Saturn	Samstag	Sabbath Day
Sun.	domingo	Domenicus, the Lord's day	dimanche	Domenicus	Sonnentag	Sun Day

Here's another good listening activity:

Phone-Y Calls

Materials needed: a telephone in the classroom

Level: Intermediate to Advanced

Preparation: Have the subject matter for the call approved by the administration.

1. Have someone call you, and then hang up. Continue the conversation as a one-sided one. Students, naturally curious, will listen with bated breath, trying to guess who's on the line, and why they called. Some ideas for calls:

    - The President of the U.S. is asking your opinion on a matter of national security. Tell him what you'd like him to do. (Pick a current topic.)

    - Someone is trying to sell you a car/house/clothing. Order it.

    - It's your father/mother. Someone in the family is sick/hurt. Make arrangements to go see them: hospital name, room number, etc.

    - The police have a family member in custody. Find out why

- It's a wrong number and they think you are a pizza place/restaurant. (Use the name of a local one.) Take their order.

And here's one that's more participation-oriented:

Win, Lose, and Draw

1. Pick several students, and put each at the board, blindfolded, with a marker or chalk.

2. Tell them to draw different parts of the body, one after the other. Other topics could be a house, a particular room in a house, a plate of food, a table with objects on it, a scene depicting a farm with animals, and so on.

3. When they are done, remove the blindfolds and reward the best (?) drawing.

4. For the next round, have the students who drew call out the parts.

Reading Activities

Readings for beginners, another area that fits under Standard 1.2, must be very basic. My classes love to do a page I took from a coloring book of a skateboarder in front of a café. In each space I have written out two numbers (not in numerals) that, when deciphered and added together, yield a number to be found in a table at the bottom that tells them what color (in the target language) to color each section. For example, two and seven make nine, which is yellow.

However, readings later in the beginning year can be more exacting. Rebus readings are a winner! A rebus replaces words with a picture. Having students read rebus stories aloud to each other practices pronunciation, vocabulary and reading skills. Another beginner-level reading activity is one that requires the reader to do certain things such as coloring a map based on what is read.

Here are some Internet sources for beginning-level reading activities:

- http://www.une.edu.ve/kids/cuentos.htm—This site has a collection of short stories in Spanish, including *Los Tres Cerditos*.

- http://www.storiestogrowby.com—Contains out-of-the-ordinary folktales from around the world, in English, that are easy to translate; or have your upper-level students translate, illustrate, and read to each other.

- http://perso.wanadoo.es/manolmar/—A site with cute rebus in Spanish. Includes the story of *Jack and the Beanstalk*, *The Magic Flute*, and several more.

♦ http://www.sep.gob.mx/libros/libro.htm—Authentic materials (textbooks, etc.) developed for Mexican children.

Intermediate-Level Activities

Intermediate students learn to apply reading strategies and other study skills to comprehend a spoken or written message. Students could be asked to listen to or read things like ads, announcements, short reports, simple poetry and prose, and telephone conversations. Selections read or heard are longer and use more complex sentence structure, but are still closely connected to every day life in the target culture (authentic). Some examples of intermediate-level activities would be to have students

♦ Read a poem and analyze the poem for similes, metaphors, rhyme scheme, etc.

♦ View a taped newscast, weather report and/or commercials before as preparation for writing and recording their own newscast, weather report or commercial

♦ Comprehend complex sentences and idiomatic expressions based upon context

♦ Translate passages accurately

♦ Begin to identify and interpret emotions or feelings in selected materials

♦ Analyze the style of a passage

Here are some ideas for intermediate activities:

I've Got a Secret

1. Have each student share a secret on paper. Possibilities include a summer activity, a junk food they're addicted to, a favorite possession, a birthmark, a city visited or in which they used to live, a favorite pet, and so on. It must be something they think no one will know, but which they are comfortable sharing with the entire class.

2. Type the statements out so that handwriting is not a clue, and have students either listen to them as you read them, or read them to themselves, and try to guess who in the group wrote that one. If the class is large, narrow down their choices to three or four people.

Fortune Cookies

Purpose: to practice the future tense, and to encourage students to wish good things for classmates

1. Put students in groups of four or five. Have each student write a fortune on a slip of paper for each of the other students in the group. Be sure to specify that it should be a fortune that would make someone happy. Remind students that a good fortune may be written in the negative (e.g., "You will not die for a long time.").

2. Have students give each other the fortunes they have written.

3. Students will then take turns reading their fortunes aloud, reacting to each after reading it. The others may react as well, or discuss the fortune before going on to the next one.

4. Have each student write their fortunes, adding one they write for themselves, and one for you (the teacher). Then have them hand these in.

Variation: Have students do steps one and two. Then go to step 4, and then have the student read them all aloud, and have the other students guess which one the student wrote for himself/herself.

Comment: This activity will be much easier if done after the students know one another fairly well so that predictions reflect interests of the student and are fairly certain to make the recipient happy.

Advanced-Level Activities

Advanced students would listen to or read both formal and informal notes, business and personal correspondence, pamphlets and brochures, news articles (both factual and opinion), songs, films and literary works of poetry or prose. They should

♦ figure out any cultural nuances including humor (irony and sarcasm are forms of humor).

♦ determine the main ideas and all significant details of a oral or written piece.

♦ identify characteristics of the selection's genre and the author's writing style.

♦ comparatively analyze two or more works.

An unusual source of authentic language is an elementary-level textbook from a country that speaks the target language! It's different enough from an American text to be able to find some cultural points as well as to see what words would be taught to a native child. Students really enjoy seeing if they can read something "real" like that.

Here are some excellent Internet sources for unedited authentic advanced-level texts available at the time of this book's publication:

- ◆ French
  - http://www.yahoo.fr—Go to "Actualités" and you'll find current events news items.
  - http://www.le-petit-bouquet.com—A daily newsletter you can subscribe to for free. Contains news, culture, and even recipes.
- ◆ German
  - http://www.uncg.edu/~lixlpurc/GIP/german_units/ UnitsCover.html—Here are ten German web units with digital exercises for levels from beginning to advanced.
  - http://www.isu.edu/~nickcrai/german.html—Col. Craig's German Links
  - http://www.dwelle.de—*Deutsche Welle* online
- ◆ Italian
  - http://www.junior.rai.it/
- ◆ Latin
  - http://www.latinteach.com/webquests.html
- ◆ Spanish
  - http://www.spanishpronto.com/news.html—glossaries and links to articles on the Web.
  - http://www.cnnenespagnol.com—CNN news articles in Spanish
  - http://www.peopleenespanol.com—*People* magazine in Spanish
  - http://www.latinamericalinks.com—Links to most of the newspapers in Latin America
- ◆ Russian
  - http://eleaston.com/rsread.html#lit—Links to Russian literature
  - http://www.russnet.org—Online exercises and resources

Standard 1.3: Presentational Communication

Students present information, concepts, and ideas to an audience of listeners or readers on a variety of topics.

This standard asks students to give presentations in the target language to a variety of listeners and/or readers, in a variety of formats: oral, written or video.

Figure 2.7 lists some of the many activities teachers commonly use as presentations/projects in their schools and communities.

Figure 2.7. Presentational Communication Activities

advertising campaign	joke	rap
anecdote	lecture	re-creation of a scene from a book or movie
ballad	lesson	riddle
campaign speech	monologue	skit
choral reading	narration	song
dance	newscast	video
demonstration	oath	weather report
documentary	oral report	
dramatization	phone call	

Beginner-Level Activities

Beginners can present

- ◆ Illustrated stories about activities or events to share with the class

- ◆ Plays, skits, or puppet shows (I can still remember being Chicken Little in a Spanish puppet show we did in fifth grade. I still have the puppet I made for this presentation.)

- ◆ Choral or individual readings from a printed source

- ◆ Poems, recited or read with appropriate expression

- ◆ Simple poems such as concrete poetry or a cinquain, illustrated and posted in the hallway

- ◆ Songs, jingles, or popular sayings

- ◆ Information about themselves

- ◆ Dances that are culturally appropriate

- ◆ Oral reports on monuments, holidays, countries or other topics

Here are some beginner-level presentation activities:

Beginners' Poems

- ◆ Diamond Poems

  Have students follow this formula:

  Noun

  2 adjectives

  3 verbs

  Phrase or sentence

  Noun that either is a synonym or an antonym of the original noun

- ◆ Calligrams

  Students select an object and write the poem about it, with the words visually creating a representation of either the object's outline, or its actual shape. For example, a poem about a tree could have the words written to form the outline of a tree, or a poem about winter ice could take the solid form of an icicle.

- ◆ Acrostics

  The poem's topic is written vertically down the left-hand side of the page, and each letter of the word is used as the beginning of a line of the poem. For beginners, have each line be an adjective or a statement that describes the word. (I also do this with students' names.)

  Example: DOG

  Dear, sweet pet

  Often playful

  Goes to find its ball.

Me Book

The first day of class, my beginners start their "Me Book" as we learn how to say our names and choose a nickname in the target language for each of them.

1. Have students count the number of family members they have: father, mother, sisters, brothers, grandparents, and pets, including anyone else they are close to, even neighbors or friends who seem

like family. (Don't let them forget themselves!) Divide that number by three, and pick up that many pieces of paper, fold in half to resemble a book, and staple in the center. (You will need a special stapler to do this.)

2. On the front, leave half the page for a picture. (I'm fortunate to have a digital camera and a color printer available; other options might be to use a Polaroid, taking several students at once, or to get a copy of their school photo or one copied from last year's yearbook.) Below the picture have students write, "My name is Firstname 'Nickname' Lastname" in the target language. Then have them number the pages, and that's all for the first day. (In my classes, these books stay in my room.)

3. As they learn new ways to describe themselves, students add those: "My nationality is ..." until they learn the family members. At that time, starting on page 3 (to have extra room for the "me" information), and beginning a third to halfway down the page, they write "My father" on one page, "My mother" on another, and so on, until all family members are represented, each on his/her own page. Below the relationship, students write, "His/her name is (name)" and "He/she is __ years old."

4. Throughout the semester, in addition to pictures (real or cut out of a magazine), information from each unit is added: for example, each person's job, favorite color, food and day of the week, season and weather, plus descriptive adjectives, both looks and personality. These are great for parent conferences, when I like to have the student present his/her book to the parents.

5. Students also make some kind of creative cover for their book, as a homework assignment. It is interesting to see what they come up with.

6. Students periodically, also, read their books to each other (a good activity to leave for a substitute) and I also have them interview each other about the books using the Inside/Outside circle method and an interview grid such as the one in Figure 2.8. The grids we use are in the target language and answers written on them are also written in the target language, of course.

Figure 2.8. Family Interview Grid

♦ What's your parent's name? ♦ How old is he/she? ♦ Is he/she tall?	♦ How old is your aunt? ♦ What is her job? ♦ Does she live in (our town)?	♦ Name a male cousin. ♦ Is he tall? blond? ♦ How old is he?
♦ Do you have brothers or sisters? ♦ Are they older or younger than you? ♦ Describe one of them:	♦ Is your grandfather a teacher? ♦ Is he interesting? ♦ What's his nationality?	♦ Is your uncle French? ♦ Is he married? ♦ Is he rich or poor?
♦ Is your female cousin in high school? ♦ What's her name? ♦ Is she nice or annoying?	♦ What's your grandmother's name? ♦ Is she fat or thin? ♦ Where does she live?	♦ Name another person in your family you haven't discussed yet. ♦ Is he/she your cousin? ♦ Is he/she an actor/actress? ♦ What is his/her nationality?

Variations:

♦ If you have lots of students likely to come from single-parent families, broken homes, or if a student recently has had a family tragedy, instead of having them do their real family, assign an "ideal" family. Bring in *People* magazine (or *Biography*, *Newsweek*, *Time*, or any other that has photos of famous people) and have them construct a book with their "ideal" family. This is high-interest when it is time to present! If I do this, I also make them justify their choice of this person: she is pretty, he is rich, they are intelligent, and so on.

♦ If you have access to magazines in the target language, have them add a French/German/Spanish family branch to their real family, by cutting out pictures of famous people and describing them. This is a good way to include Culture (Standard 2) in this.

Readers Theater

Studies show that listening comprehension shoots up for students who hear stories several times a week for a short period. Why not involve students in doing the reading?

This is also great for performances for foreign language club meetings, or other school or community groups. Here's how I do it:

1. Divide students in groups and assign each a chapter, a poem, or a short story. (This is a favorite activity of mine at Halloween with scary stories, always high-interest!)

2. Each student in the group gets a portion of the story, and several days to practice his/her part. Remind them to read as expressively and meaningfully as possible.

3. The group should also discuss how to enhance their reading: props, costumes, sound effects, voice pitch or quality (for example, to sound old), and so on. They should also prepare a couple of open-ended discussion questions for after the reading, for example, what they liked, funny or scary parts, what happens next.

4. On the day of the reading, introduce the selection to the class. Preteach any important words (such as pumpkin or ghost, for Halloween). Then have the students take turns reading their selection. As one reads, everyone else in the class must pay attention. When the first student finishes, he/she passes the text to the next person to read, so that everyone is listening to the performer.

Variations:

♦ Have students self-select their items for reading. In this way, you are assured of their interest in that selection.

♦ Change this from individual readings to choral reading: a group of students would read the selection simultaneously. This requires even more practice on their part than an individual reading, and a weaker or timid reader will feel more comfortable performing in a group setting.

♦ Make the text available to every member of the class. (Use overhead transparencies, PowerPoint or a large paper chart rather than a small text so that students look at the performers rather than down at their desks.) This is especially good if the text is challenging, or if a large number of students seem to be visual learners (although props and costumes will help those students as well).

♦ If the story has a clear, repetitious refrain (such as the "Run, run, as fast as you can; You can't catch me, I'm the Gingerbread Man!") have audience participation included in the performance. This is easier if what they are to say is displayed visually, at least for the first few times in the story.

♦ Include a cultural element. Many third-world storytellers stop from time to time and say a standard phrase to which the audience must reply. In French, this is seen in the African expression "Cric? Crac!" found in stories, and seen in the film *Sugar Cane Alley.* This adds an element of authentic culture as well as an audience participation element, and keeps students listening. It also offers a brief pause and chance to "digest" what has been heard so far in the story.

Intermediate-Level Activities

Intermediate-level students might do some or all of the following:

♦ Taped or videotaped messages to share locally (local radio station) or with peers at school (other classes or over school address system) on items of local interest

♦ A fashion show

♦ A weathercast

♦ A mock interview of a famous person

♦ Written reports on cultural events, artifacts, geographical items

♦ A monologue or retelling of a story

♦ A question-and-answer session

♦ An original poem, presented to an audience

From the intermediate level, we often have students perform things they have written themselves. Here is a good teacher resource to use when assigning writing assignments:

http://teacher.scholastic.com—This is a great Teacher Resource center from Scholastic Books. It includes an Online Activities center dealing with reading and writing activities, with well-known authors contributing and lots of structured guidance to help in writing folk stories, biographies, news articles, and other types of writing. Although they are in English, they are applicable and easily converted to activities to use in any foreign language creative writing endeavor.

Here are some intermediate-level presentation activities:

Prop Talk

In this activity, students prepare and present/explain a drawing, Power-Point, or a poster.

Have students create illustrated scenes or stories that they present either in pairs or individually. For example, during a unit on household chores, ask them to draw a cross-section of a house, with different family members or friends doing various chores. (This portion is usually assigned as homework.)

In class, give them about five minutes to prepare a two- to three-sentence speech. For example, with the chores presentation, they might identify the people in the picture, tell what room they are in and say what they are doing, using the targeted vocabulary in that unit and the verb tense of your choice.

Here's some other props ideas:

- Fill several bags with one household item and one index card in each. On the card, you have written helpful vocabulary words to use with that item. Give each student or group a bag, and allow two minutes to come up with every use they can think of for that item (in the target language). This can be done as a written or an oral activity. After time has elapsed, have them return the item and card to the bag. After three or four exchanges, students must really show creativity to come up with new ideas. For instance, if given a shoelace, they after first suggesting tying it, they might suggest using it as a belt or hairband, a keychain or bracelet, a book mark, a glasses holder, a necklace, and so on.

- Assign students to bring in an object with great personal meaning, and have them share the story of the day they got it as well as what it means to them. (This practices narration in the various past tenses, and could be done written or orally.)

- Have students bring an ordinary object with them but one that they don't normally bring to class. Tell them this object has special powers, much like some of James Bond's weapons (a wristwatch that contains a laser, a belt that doubles as a sword, and so on.) Give them a few minutes to prepare, and have them tell what the object seems to be, what it really is, and what they will do with it (practices the future tense).

- Bring in old, mismatched shoes (your own or garage sale "finds"). Give each student a shoe and have each tell five facts about the person who it belongs to,

- Purchase several strings of the plastic keys that infants use for teething. Give each student a key, and, after a few minutes, have each tell who they think it belongs to and what it will open. (Tell them that creativity is a big part of the grade, or these will be boring.)

- Give each student a piece of candy or gum. Then tell them to either eat it, save it, or trade it for something different. Then ask them to tell what they originally received, and what they did with it. (This practices the imperfect and the preterit).

Car Talk

In an effort to have more male-oriented activities (in response to student evaluations), instead of doing an ad for make-up, shampoo, and so on, and to practice command forms of verbs, my level 2 students create a new car, with a commercial to market it. They perform the commercial for the rest of the class (and, with permission, for our school in-house television after the daily announcements).

After the ads have been presented, other steps can extend the experience:

1. Involve students in discussing favorite car ads. Develop a list of advertising strategies commonly used. Ours usually include

   Adventure (e.g., rugged landscape, driving on a race track or in an exotic location)

   Sex (e.g., pretty girl driving)

   Humor

   Safety features or other unique features (roominess)

   Special spokesperson (famous actor or spokesperson like Joe Isuzu)

2. Students must develop a name for their car, truck, or van in the target language, plus some unique or unusual feature, and then work on a marketing strategy that includes a slogan/motto/concept involving a verb in the command form (such as "Drive an X" or "Buy a Y"), a poster, and a skit (live or on video).

   Figure 2.9 shows the rubric checklist I give students for this project.

3. Involve students in setting guidelines for this project in addition to those above! Here are some additional considerations:

   How much of the target language should be used on the poster? One phrase? Two sentences?

   Define "creativity." (I always tell my students that the only difference between an A and a B is creativity.)

   How many sentences must all participants speak?

   What else is important?

Figure 2.9. Car Talk Project Checklist

Deadline date: _____

Requirement:	*Comment:*
Product name:	_____ (1 pt.) Must be in (target language)
Poster:	_____ (1 pt) Name of vehicle prominently displayed
	_____ (1 pt) Has a slogan/message/concept
	_____ (1 pt) Colorful
	_____ (1 pt) Neatly done
	_____ (1 pt) No errors in spelling
	_____ (1 pt) No errors in grammar
Ad:	_____ (1 pt) Everyone speaks
	_____ (1 pt) Slogan/message/concept repeated in ad
	_____ (1 pt) No errors in pronunciation

---

4. Grading: Before the final project is presented, I give students a copy of the grading sheet I will use. It usually is a checklist like the one in Figure 2.9, with the addition of things mutually agreed upon in Step 3. But I like to keep students actively involved during the presentations, so I have them help me grade them. (Students generally are much more critical and more harsh in grading than I am.) I give them the same form I'm using, and we all fill one out. I average the class's grades (dropping the lowest and highest evaluation, as is done in some real competitions) and make them average that with my grade for the final grade, so their input is worth 50 percent, and is equal to mine.

Family Brag Book

When doing our family unit review at Level 2, because students have done a "Me Book" in the first year, I introduce my own family, whose roots are in various parts of the world, and about whom some of my knowledge is limited; I know nothing about my paternal grandfather, for example. I tell them that it is time to find out about and celebrate our families, by making an illustrated story about one family member who is truly wonderful.

Have students ask about their families and choose a person who is or was a good person: someone who came to the U.S. to find a better life, someone who bakes birthday cakes for elderly shut-ins, or who saved a person from choking in a restaurant, or won a prize …

Then, the student should prepare and illustrate one of the following about that person:

♦ a story

♦ a storyboard

♦ a poem

♦ a slide show or PowerPoint

♦ a rap or song

♦ a video

Involve students in creating the requirements and grading system for this project.

Pick a day and invite family members to the presentation. (If possible, ask the person chosen to be profiled; I ask ahead of time and purchase a flower for the student to give that person.) This can be a truly memorable day, and the presentations are always very interesting.

Poetry Soothes …

Poems are a great way to have students express themselves creatively, and particularly lend themselves to public presentations or displays on bulletin boards. Here are a few suggestions of poems to try.

♦ Word Sack Poems

This activity was suggested to me by the magnetic Refrigerator Poetry kits sold in major bookstores. Put selected vocabulary words (make sure nouns, adjectives, adverbs and verbs are all represented) into a sack. Have students take two "pinches" of words, then lay them out on a blank sheet of paper and move them about to create a poem. They may, of course, add determiners and auxiliary words for it to make better sense, as well as perhaps another "pinch" of words if needed. After creating the poem, they then copy it onto the paper, and illustrate it. These may be read aloud or posted for students' enjoyment.

♦ Experience-Based Poetry

Give students the handout shown in Figure 2.10.

Figure 2.10. Experience-Based Poetry Form

1. List the five most memorable experiences you've had this month.
    List the emotions you felt during this experience.

_____

_____

_____

_____

2. Look over the five events, and put a star next to the one that is most important to you.

3. Write fifteen words or phrases that come to your mind about the event you have selected.

_____   _____   _____

_____   _____   _____

_____   _____   _____

_____   _____   _____

_____   _____   _____

4. Now, organize the fifteen words that you wrote above to create a poem.

♦ Ideas for Presenting an Original Poem

- Prepare a list of vocabulary for the class that will help them to better understand the poem.

- Prepare a list of questions about the poem that can be used to begin a discussion about the content, the interpretation, the significance, or the theme of the poem.

Advanced-Level Activities

To all previously acquired skills, advanced level students will add persuasive presentations. These are opinionated, editorializing activities such as the following:

♦ Research-based analysis of a current event

♦ A student-written newscast or newsletter

♦ An opinion speech, such as describing and justifying a personal preference

♦ Re-creating a scene from a play or a movie, in the target language

♦ Analysis of a literary work for cultural nuances, style, etc.

♦ A debate: who had the most interesting day yesterday? (et cetera)

♦ Humor: jokes, anecdotes or stories

♦ Very advanced creative writing (which also may be performed or read aloud)

Here are some advanced-level activities for Standard 1.3 Presentational:

Newscast or Newspaper

1. Divide the class into groups of three or four. Have them meet and decide what sort of newscast they want to present. Who is their audience (age, education, interests, lifestyle, geographic location, political leanings)? This will affect their choice of news items.

2. Each group summarizes its decisions on a form (see Figure 2.11, p. 50) to give to the teacher.

3. Teacher will assign events to be covered (for example, school events, a certain historic time period, current events in a target language location) because then a larger number of events can be dealt with later in the discussion phase.

4. Reporters decide how to gather the news (what type of information to seek, where to seek it, and who will do it). They add this to the form, and return it to the teacher, and then begin gathering information.

5. The group writes a report on the event assigned. Sources should be quoted or given credit. Report is handed in to the teacher with their evaluation of how well they think they addressed their intended audience in this article.

6. The teacher edits the articles and returns them to the group for corrections.

7. The teacher puts all the articles together and makes copies for the class or the groups videotape their articles as newscasts.

8. The class reads the articles or views the newscasts.

9. The group meets one more time, completes the final evaluation portion of the form, and hands it in.

Figure 2.11. Newspaper Articles

Group: _____   _____

_____ and _____

TARGET:

Definition of readers _____

TOPIC assigned by teacher: _____

Source	Type of info	Who's doing it
_____	_____	_____
_____	_____	_____
_____	_____	_____
_____	_____	_____

How we attempted to select and present information for our target audience: _____

_____

FILL OUT PORTION BELOW AFTER VIEWING:

Our article was: (circle one)   better   as good as   worse   than the others.

Grade we think our effort deserved: _____

and why: _____

We did well at: _____

We could have done this better/more: _____

Here is an advanced activity I find students enjoy:

Chapter 23 and a Half

1. Pick a work of literature your students are studying or have studied and know quite well. I have done this with *Don Quixote*, *The Little Prince*, *Candide*, and *Le Petit Nicolas*.

2. Analyze the author's style, common words and phrases used, the tone of the work, and the structure of a typical chapter. Also discuss characterization and plot. For example, Don Quixote always has his sidekick Sancho Panza, just as Candide always has a companion.

3. Then, assign the writing of another chapter, with an accompanying illustration. The rubric (Figure 2.12) is a simple checklist (10 points,

multiply each by an equal amount to get the total points you would like).

Figure 2.12. Rubric for Chapter 23 and a Half

Yes   *No*

_____   _____   Setting is clear (time and place).

_____   _____   Main character is consistent with character in book: personality, looks and actions.

_____   _____   Sidekick is described and contributes to action in chapter.

_____   _____   Dialogue is used, with diction and phrases common to book chapters.

_____   _____   Actions are logical and typical for the setting and characters.

_____   _____   New chapter begins and ends like a typical chapter.

_____   _____   There is an obvious theme/message/moral to this chapter.

_____   _____   Target language is grammatical and spelled correctly (± 3 errors)

_____   _____   Illustration is neat and large enough to see easily.

_____   _____   Illustration fits content of the chapter.

Actually, I usually have my students list what is typical and what would be important to include. I "lead" them in discussion until their list looks close to the one above. Sometimes they have other details they would like included. It's important that they should feel "ownership" in the requirements for this assignment and that the discussion leads to a good understanding of the structure, style, and tone of the book.

Here is another, more impromptu activity:

Almost-Mime Scenes

1. Ask students, either individually or in groups of two to four to create a short scene using both actions and words to convey one of the following ideas:

arriving	finding something	protesting	wanting
enjoying something	permitting	teaching	ending an activity
leaving a place	taking over	death	having a problem
searching	birth	growing old	reuniting
beginning a relationship	first new car/bike	refusing	wistfulness

2. As students watch each other perform, the watchers write down their guess which concept is being portrayed.

3. Afterward, have students check their guesses with each group, complimenting good performances and giving suggestions for improvements in those that weren't as clear.

3

Standard 2: Cultures

> ♦ Gain Knowledge and Understanding of Other Cultures
>
> • Standard 2.1: Students demonstrate an understanding of the relationship between the practices and perspectives of the culture studied.
>
> • Standard 2.2: Students demonstrate an understanding of the relationship between the products and perspectives of the culture studied.

Culture is the second most important component of foreign language instruction. Students cannot truly master a language until they have mastered the cultural contexts in which the language occurs, and so knowledge of the culture of the target language is essential.

Instead of the two-part "big-C, little-c" culture we are most used to (big-C being high/serious art, music and literature and little-c making crafts, cooking and other everyday activities), the people who produced the national standards have chosen to divide this into three parts: perspectives, practices and products.

The practices category is familiar territory: social behaviors such as greetings; holidays such as Mardi Gras, Dia de los Muertos, and Oktoberfest; ceremonies such as coming-of-age ceremonies; and rites such as marriages and graveside practices. A culture's political and educational systems would also fit in here. Although they are products of an unwritten but deeply ingrained system of beliefs and expectations in that culture, they are certainly visible cultural manifestations. The essential long-term result of teaching a practice would be that a student is aware of and knowledgeable about the practice and therefore is able to participate in it if necessary.

Products are the easiest to understand, because most teachers and texts concentrate on this. It includes not just the big-C masterpieces of architecture, art, cinema, and literature, but everyday items such as rolling pins, chopsticks, wedding veils, and boiled peanuts. Products are also intangible items, especially music (popular, traditional, or classical). The goal of presenting a product is that a student should recognize the product and be aware of its role in the culture.

Perspectives is the newer addition. This refers to commonly held values, folk ideas, shared attitudes, and widely held assumptions, opinions and attitudes, whether these be openly expressed or hidden. In other words, it is the *world view* of a culture, the answers to the questions "Why do they do this like that?" or, "How can they possibly think that?" Perspectives lessons, therefore, are potentially difficult. Many themes dealing with cultural perspectives—attitudes toward family, life and death, work, or corruption; concepts of personal honor, the role of religion in society, social class structure and its consequences; or attitudes towards animals—are difficult to convey in the target language to middle- and high-school students, and risk creating stereotypes as well. Tricky territory!

How to Inject Culture into Communication Projects

It's fairly easy to convert a project from Standard 1 (Communication) to include this standard as well.

Make "cultural authenticity" part of every evaluation rubric. If it's a skit, insist on culturally authentic body language, phrases or expressions, and pronunciation. If it's something like the "Me Book" in Chapter 2, require students to list everyone's "appellido." When cooking, assign groups to a particular country and have them research typical dishes. Have students scan ads in a target language publication before designing ads of their own, or watch a native language newscast before planning and presenting one.

Ideally, culture would be part of any lesson, not the main lesson itself. If you are teaching language in context and using culturally appropriate texts, you will be teaching culture. For example, when you do the verb "to go," use a real city. Learn its streets, stores, and tourist sites (churches, museums, and so on).

The biggest cultural artifact of any culture is its language. Use the Internet and have them read, read, and read some more; then discuss and learn. It is a valuable source of authentic material.

Look for similarities and don't focus on differences! Students usually immediate detect (and criticize) differences between the target language culture and their own. Help them find similarities, and the material they learn will be stored in long term memory! Let's face it: material culture is becoming more and more similar around the world. An American living in Madrid, Paris, Rome, or Berlin will find McDonald's, blue jeans, American music and movies, computers, cell phones, cable TV, a modern subway system, discussions over where to build the new airport, and so on. Finding familiar things will help make students want to visit that place more, as well as make them more accepting of the differences that exist. You'll find more on this topic in Chapter 4.

Debunk stereotypes with authenticity: most Spanish-speaking countries do *not* eat spicy food, most French people do *not* own a beret, and so on.

Standard 2.1: Practices and Perspectives

Students demonstrate an understanding of the relationship between the practices and perspectives of the culture studied.

This standard focuses on the practices that are traditional in a culture. Cultural practices generally refer to patterns of behavior accepted by a society. In short, they represent the knowledge of what to do, when, and where.

Typical practices taught are:

♦ Identification and use of appropriate oral expressions or nonverbal expressions

Oral expressions include greetings, leave-takings, and courtesy for basic school and social situations: please, thank you, excuse me, response to a sneeze, or statements when serving food (such as *bon appétit*). An example of a nonverbal expression would be a word like "um" or a swift exhalation or inhalation of breath. This appropriateness would also refer to knowing when to switch between formal and informal language.

♦ Identification and use of culturally appropriate gestures and facial expressions, and situations in which they are used

This includes things such as table manners, eye contact, interpersonal space, and touching rules (for example, conversational distance), and bows such as are common in Japan or China.

♦ Appropriate manner of dress for target language cultures, or different regions of a country

Dress may also be differentiated according to age, social level, and historical era. (The latter especially applies to Latin).

♦ Typical occupations found in areas that speak the target language

♦ Popular sports and their rules, such as soccer, pétanque, and others

Don't just study them, actually play them! We built a pétanque court at our school. We wear our own team shirts when we invite area high schools and eighth-grade classes over to play. The French Club will sometimes challenge the Spanish Club, too.

♦ Business practices

Examples include handshakes and greetings, salutations and closes for business letters, job interviews (mostly for upper levels)

♦ Educational systems

Include schools, what is studied, days and a typical schedule, and so on.

♦ Political systems of countries speaking the target language

Examples include political parties, elections, and the structure and operation of various governmental and legal systems.

♦ Family roles and relationships

♦ Methods of telling time

♦ Holidays and how they are celebrated

♦ Age-appropriate activities such as games, songs, and rhymes

See the activities described in this chapter.

♦ Study of areas of the world where the target language is spoken

♦ Common methods of conflict resolution

♦ Typical uses for leisure time

These can be varied by age and social standing if appropriate.

♦ Humor and satire in the target language

Examples include cartoons, comedies from theater (like Molière), movies, newspaper articles, and other resources.

♦ Past practices

Slavery is an example (again, particularly appropriate for Latin).

Start Small

Children are pretty much the same worldwide. They all have games, songs and other activities that are great to use in the classroom to learn or practice vocabulary, pronunciation, illustrate or introduce new verb tenses, and so on.

Some children's activities that make great classroom additions are described on the Internet at the following sites:

♦ Tongue twisters (Zungenbrecher/Trabalenguas/Virelangues)

The site at http://www.uebersetzung.at/twister/ has the largest collection of these that I've ever seen.

♦ Games in general

The site at http://www.geocities.com/Athens/Styx/6504/games.html has games from several different countries around the world.

♦ Jump rope rhymes

Besides the above site, French jump rope rhymes can be found at http://www.momes.net. German children's rhymes and songs are at http://www.decus.de:8080/wsz/kidrh/krd.htmlx.

Here are some Spanish jump rope rhymes:

Una, dos y tres, pluma, tintero y papel para escribir una carta a mi querido Miguel. En la carta le decía recuerdo para tu tía que está comiendo judías en un barril de lejía.	Una y dos, Me calzo y me voy. Tres y cuatro, a la puerta llamo. Cinco y seis, palitos hallé Siete y ocho, un castillo formó Nueve y diez, gallinas y pollitos están a mis pies.	Te convido ¿A qué? A café ¿A qué hora? A las tres, uno, dos y tres. Entra rosa. color de mariposa, Sal clavel, color de moscatel.
Té, chocolate y café para mi tío Manuel. Una, dos y tres, pluma, tintero y papel para escribir una carta a mi hermanita Isabel.	En la plaza Mayo se rifará un gato; a la una, a las dos, a las tres y a las cuatro.	Que una, que dos, a la lata, al latero, a las hijas del hojalatero. Que viva la lata, Que viva el latero, Que viva las hijas del hojalatero.

♦ Songs are great to use.

Try translations of familiar songs ("Old McDonald," "This Old Man"), Christmas carols or other holiday songs, both translated and traditional, from *Adeste Fidelis* to the present, and any other traditional tunes. I can still sing almost 20 carols in Latin from my high-school days long, long ago.

There is a web site at http://www.tsl.state.tx.us/ld/projects/ninos/ songsrhymes.html where you can find little kids' songs in Spanish. It also tells the history of the songs and has RealAudio versions that you can listen to, with words accompanying it, and which you can download and save on your computer.

For French, try http://www.momes.net for authentic songs and rhymes.

♦ Poems to memorize

Pick a literary poem that children in the target language country would all know, or use a Mother Goose rhyme or even something like the Pledge of Allegiance in the target language. My students just love to go home and rattle off something they've memorized, to impress siblings, parents, and relatives.

The following are creative culture units that deal with practices:

Weights and Measures:
An Internet Lesson in Culture

Language: French but easily transferable to other languages.

Level: Upper Beginner or Lower Intermediate

1. Send students to read recipes on the Internet. The addresses I currently use are http://www.chez.com/recettesfaciles (French site, translates "easy recipes"), http://www.arts-culinaires.com (Canadian site), or, for beginners, http://www.epicurious.com (in English, but has great recipes).

    For Spanish, try Recetas favoritas de España at http://www. xmission.com/~dderhale/recetas.html, or, from Mexico, http://home.att.net/~enrique.houston/cocina.html.

    For German, see http://kochbuch.unix-ag.uni-kl.de/bin/ kategorie.

2. Have students copy quantities seen in recipes: how much flour, salt, sugar, apples, and so on are used. Have them deductively determine what these expressions mean in English.

3. Send them to a metric conversion site to determine the English equivalents.

4. Ask them to choose a recipe that sounds good, and translate it.

5. Ask volunteers to prepare some for the class (or you can), or for their families.

6. For those who do this, require a brief opinion survey on whether they liked it or not. See Figure 3.1. I give extra credit to students who prepare the recipe they have chosen; I do not require this. Students may prepare the recipe at home and have their parents verify the work.

7. Discussion afterward would center on general impressions of French food, and whether we should change to the metric system.

Figure 3.1. Recipe Form

Name of student: _____

Recipe prepared: _____

Date prepared: _____

Parent's signature: _____

Circle the appropriate words or phrases:

We	did	did not	have the ingredients needed on hand.
If no, the ingredients	were	were not	easy to find.
The recipe was	easy	difficult	to prepare.
It tasted	great	good	okay

News in Depth

Language: Any

Level: Intermediate to Advanced

Current events are always a good way to reflect upon the practices and perspectives of the culture being studied. To find current foreign news, try the Yahoo site for the country, for example www.yahoo.mx, www.yahoo.es, www.yahoo.fr, www.yahoo.de, and so on. Present an actual news story to your students using one or more of these steps:

1. Write the headline on the overhead or the board, with students pronouncing it as you write. Ask them to pick out cognates or words they know, and to guess at the content of the article.

2. Teach them key words necessary for comprehension of the article, and have them practice using them in a sentence.

3. Go over any basic geographical or historical events necessary to understand the story.

4. Then, give students the unedited story to read for understanding. Ask them to either underline all the words they DO know, and then pick five words they'd like help with (this way they won't focus on the length of the selection, but just on the difficult spots); or have them underline all the words they think are important in the story, and choose three for you to help them with.

5. After determining the main thrust of the story, have a discussion of the cultural perspective, and perhaps go to the Internet, either to survey keypals as to whether they have this attitude, or to look for further examples.

This sort of activity can be a great vocabulary builder as well as an authentic reading text and a cultural artifact. The story doesn't have to be about the target language culture, just in the target language and it should reflect an attitude of that culture. For example, I've found the French are usually amused at American outrage over the infidelities of various celebrities and that, though they have no royalty of their own, are inordinately occupied with the ins-and-outs of the lives of other countries' royalty.

And finally, here is a project that deals with both a practice and a product:

Crazy About Cascarones:
A Spanish Cultural Event

Language: Spanish

Level: Any

A *cascarone* is a decorated eggshell filled with confetti that is broken over someone's head at a party. It is an interesting, fast, and easy craft that even small children can do, which is used in a high-interest activity after it is finished. You can do make these yourself, or have students make them, depending on the age and likelihood they'll follow your instructions.

1. Use a darning needle or some sharp, thin tool to poke a small hole in the narrower end of an egg, and make a larger hole (approximately dime-sized) in the other end of the egg. I like to use a large corsage pin with a big "pearl" ball on the end. Gently blow through the smaller hole, holding the egg over a bowl or bucket so the insides are emptied. Then rinse the shell out, and allow it to dry for a day. Make an omelet or something eggy with the insides!

2. The next day, use a rolled-paper cone or a small funnel and pour in confetti (glitter or flour would work, too but make MUCH more of a mess to clean up). Use purchased confetti from a paper supply store, or make your own with a hole punch and colored paper. Then paste

a small square of tissue paper over the larger hole to seal the egg. Allow this to dry for about a day. I have students write their names on their eggs.

3. Decorating the eggs further is nice, but optional. Decorations can be drawings, paint, or small squares of tissue paper. Make sure that whatever coating is used is thin so the eggs don't require a lot of force to break them! That could be painful. Sample eggs and designs, as well as historical details and party suggestions can be found on the Internet at the following addresses:

http://www.cascaroncrazy.com/cascarones.htm

http://www.aeb.org/recipes/calendar/2000/april.html

http://latinoculture.about.com/library/weekly/aa041101a.htm

Standard 2.2:
Products and Perspectives

Students demonstrate an understanding of the relationship between the products and perspectives of the culture studied.

Products come in many different forms, both tangible (a painting or a piece of literature for big-C culture, or a pair of chopsticks or some clothing for little-C) and intangible (for example, an oral product such as a story or a ritual, or a political or educational system). Whatever the product may be, though, there are basic beliefs, values, or perspectives of that culture that both cause and explain that product's existence, and most products have an accompanying cultural practice that can be discussed.

The Products category can be broken down into several different types of products:

♦ Written—big-C ones such as literature and poetry, and little-C ones like advertising, fairy tales and other types of folklore.

Don't forget humor as well—puns, double entendres, riddles and other simple forms are very popular with students. Even looking at cultural connotations of common words, phrases and idioms can be an important thing to do. I've had some interesting discussions regarding the French saying, "The apple doesn't fall far from the tree," which places responsibility for a child's behavior on all members of the family.

♦ Artistic—big-C art like that in museums, and simple arts and crafts, including cartoons; music and cinema as well as photography.

- Social—laws, the educational and welfare systems, economic bodies such as the European Economic Community (EEC), and political systems.

- Technological—inventions and discoveries as well as Internet resources.

- Historical—the *Who's Who* of famous people in the target language culture, as well as events that influenced the world or the development of the language itself.

- Gender-oriented—women's roles and their contributions to the culture. These are often overlooked in a standard text and should not be left out.

Typically, products are usually done in project form rather than as a lesson/lecture. Here are some examples of common classroom events that fall into the Products category:

- Identifying and describing a variety of objects: toys, dress, buildings, foods, tools (including tableware).

- Identifying and interpreting the cultural message found in signs, advertisements, symbols, and so on in the target language. This can also include historical cultures, such as learning Mayan math, Roman slavery laws, or samurai dress.

- Making examples of crafts typical of the target culture: molas, ojos de Dio, worry dolls, masks, bark paintings, Roman mosaic panels, stained glass, Christmas ornaments, and many more!

- Viewing or creating maps that illustrate products of the country and the areas that produce various examples of these products, or maps that identify geographical features of the country, and discussing their influence on the local culture.

- Examining and/or creating realia scrapbooks: product labels, magazine ads, movie ads, newspaper articles, and so on.

- Creating and/or wearing traditional dress (toga, serape, obi sash, and so on).

Here is a sample project for a French class:

Masks We Wear:
A Franco-African Practice and Perspective

Language: French
Level: Intermediate

This is a good activity to do in February, which is National Black History Month.

Read Léopold Senghor's poem "Masques" (easily available from many texts or on the Internet). Discuss the poem. Have upper-level students write a short essay on a mask they show the world.

Look at typical African masks, using art books, actual examples (I was fortunate to have a colleague who'd lived in Kenya), or the Internet, and make some masks. Masks are easily made from flat brown paper grocery bags, paper plates, or plastic milk jugs: cut off the tops and bottoms as well as the part with the handle, and shape the remainder, cutting eye holes and covering it with tissue paper or masking tape, rubbing on shoe polish and decorating. I generally make most of this a homework project.

Display the finished masks. You can also have an art teacher judge them, and give prizes if desired. These really brighten the classroom and are good conversation topics as well as an opportunity to review descriptive vocabulary.

A Few Comments on Rubrics for Grading Projects

I am a firm believer in letting students set the requirements for a project grade of A, so I do not include a rubric for the above masks. Usually what I do is bring out some masks from a previous year (both good, mediocre, and bad ones) and ask them to tell me which are the best, and why. I list their description of the "best" characteristics on the board or the overhead projector, and when we are done, I tell them that this is an A mask. I either have them copy these down, or promise to give it to them the next day. Then we agree on which points are least necessary, refining the list to B and C descriptions.

There are many advantages to doing this. First, because they themselves suggested the characteristics, they are more likely to remember what is needed. Even if I've had to prompt them to include a characteristic I feel is important, as soon as a student agrees that it's important, it becomes "theirs" and they forget it was my idea! (For example, a gentle prompt that asks them to take ownership such as "Doesn't anyone feel that it's important to have the mask cover the person's entire face?" would be more effective than saying, "I think the mask should cover the entire face!") Second, students feel ownership in the rubric—and this transfers to the entire project, amazingly—as it isn't just imposed upon them by the teacher. They have chosen the parameters to fulfill. Finally, by seeing examples of previous A masks, the achievers in the group are spurred to produce as good a mask, or better if possible, and the products get better every year. So, this is why I will not give rubrics for the projects suggested in this chapter.

New Twists on the Usual Projects

Of course, because projects are the most commonly taught types of cultural presentations, we all have our favorite units. Here are a few suggestions on ways to approach the standard cultural topics.

Famous People

So You Wanna Be a Hero ...

If possible, find a list (usually major magazines do this sort of survey around New Year's Day) of the nation's top 50 people. This will give your students a good cultural perspective on the people who are currently living that the culture values. Give students this list, and see how many they can identify. Then, assign the unknowns as research for a brief report on what they've done to make the list. Seeing a list of national heroes (living or dead) would give a similar perspective: does the culture value sports, the arts, political power, or all equally? What sorts of heroes (and heroines) predominate on the list?

Body Count

Language: Any

Level: Whenever famous people are learned

We all teach about famous historical figures, artists and musicians, writers, and other people from the target language culture. There are many ways to review these. Game show formats such as *What's My Line? The Weakest Link, Who Wants to Be a Millionaire?* and so on are popular with students. Here's another option that generates large visuals to put in the hall (and encourage others to guess who they represent. I adapted this from a popular activity we do when we study body parts.

1. Divide students into groups. One student volunteer will lie down and be outlined by the others much like the police chalk outlines of bodies we see on TV or in the movies. (But we use crayons or markers.) Then the student stands up, and the group uses the resulting outline as follows.

2. Either allow students to choose what person to draw, or assign them a subject. Then they draw characteristics (hairstyle, glasses, props) onto the outline that might serve as clues to the identity of the person, labeling them in the target language, of course. Examples of props include a book for a writer, sports equipment for an athlete, a microphone for a singer. A musical-note dialogue bubble like in a cartoon could indicate a singer.

3. At the feet of the outline, add more hints, in sentence form: I live in (country or city). I like (people, ideas, etc.), and so on, still in the target language, of course.

4. Post the resulting drawings on the wall, and have students guess who each drawing represents.

Music

Music Soothes the Savage ... Classroom

Language: Any

Level: Any

What student does not like music? Who can't remember ad jingles from TV or radio? Make the cultural experience authentic, enjoyable, and memorable with some music. Musical selections can be chosen for many reasons, including the following:

♦ The song uses a grammar concept being studied in class. Examples would be the imperfect or subjunctive. If the song uses lots of irregulars, great! It will fix these more firmly in students' heads as they memorize the song.

♦ It's very difficult to sing with an accent. I attended a very interesting presentation at a recent Central States Conference that demonstrated that students who spoke with very heavy accents, when singing, lost their accents. So, even singing a "Hello, how are you?" song you've made up to, say, the tune of "Mary Had a Little Lamb" will improve students' pronunciation.

♦ Songs may be used to review vocabulary or grammar concepts. Take out all the verbs in the song, and have students write them in, in the correct tense. Then listen to the song and they can check their answers. With vocabulary, take out key words, put them at the top of the page with blanks in the lyrics where they belong, and have students decide where they should go. This is a good reading activity as well as a review, and when they check their answers, it becomes a listening activity, too.

♦ Songs are kinetic activities by nature. Find a song that tells a story, and act it out as you sing it. Or assign students to invent choreography for any song, teach it to the class in the target language, and perform it (taking it up a notch to another national standard).

♦ Songs can be important parts of other cultural events, especially holidays. The Mexican custom of Las Posadas (caroling door-to-door—with tambourines, guitars and accordions as well as singers—during the Christmas season and enjoying snacks together afterward) is a delightful custom that would be easy to convert to a classroom-to-classroom activity. (This could even be done school-to-school in a campus where the high school and middle school are close together.)

Music Resources

Lately, it seems quite easy to purchase Latin American music in almost any big chain music store, so Spanish teachers should find it quite easy to get current music their students will like. A collection of sites for "Music for Teaching Spanish" can be found at http://eleaston.com/sp_music.html or you can try www.musicalspanish.com.

French music is a bit more difficult. To find out what's currently popular, I go to an online radio station such as http://www.rtl.fr (Choose "le hit") or http://www.nrj.fr. Then check out the words to see if they are okay for classroom use. For the words to the songs, the best resource is http://www.paroles.net/ but also try http://www.math.umn.edu/~foursov/chansons/ and http://site.ifrance.com/leparolier/.

A good site for children's and Québécois music is http://www.caslt.org/research/musicf.htm for use online. To purchase music, try Canada, as their merchandise (CDs and videos) are on the American system and will work here. One place to look is at http://www.archambault.ca/store/default.asp.

Food

Try new things! Offer students a taste of plantain chips, turron, artichokes, snails, or Liederkrans ... then ask them, Did you try the food? and have them respond. Beginners could use one of several choices on the board, such as:

Yes, I tried it. I loved it; give me more! (and give them more)

Yes, I tried it, unfortunately. Yuck!

More advanced classes could be asked to compare it to something else, What did it taste like? Would you eat it again?

Dispelling Common Myths

Language: Spanish or French

Format: Discussion

Level: In English, beginning; if done in target language, Intermediate

Because one of the biggest hurdles to overcome in teaching culture is to avoid stereotypes, it is important to survey your class for common stereotypes about the target language culture, and discuss them, using your own experiences and/or visual support materials to dispel them. Here are some common, but wrong, ideas about food from these two cultures:

- ♦ Spanish—Concentrating too much on a single Spanish-speaking culture and its traditions can create difficulties for students who go to a different culture, as customs and vocabulary can vary widely. Try to expose your students to as many different cultures as possible. Figure 3.2 summarizes beliefs and truths about Spanish food.

Figure 3.2. Beliefs and Truths about Spanish Food

Beliefs	*Truths*
• Taco Bell is authentic Mexican food.	• Mexican food has many regional varieties. • Mexican food prepared in the United States is altered to please American taste buds.
• Spanish food is like Mexican food.	• The food of most Spanish-speaking countries is *not* spicy.
• Food words mean the same thing in any Spanish-speaking country.	• The word "tortilla" in Spain refers to an omelet, not a flat bread made of corn or wheat. In Spain, a sandwich is a "bocadillo," and in other countries, it's an "emparedado" or a "sandwich." • Meal times vary a great deal from country to country. So do the names of meals: the word for breakfast in one can have a different meaning (or no meaning) elsewhere.
• Everyone drinks milk with a meal.	• Even children may drink wine at dinner, usually with water added.
• A typical meal will include tacos or burritos.	• Fish and seafood are much more important to the general diet than in the United States.
• There is always salt on the table.	• In Spain, fresh lemon is more available than salt and pepper as a table condiment.

- ♦ French—As with Spanish, concentrating too much on a single French-speaking culture and its traditions can create difficulties for students who go to a different culture, as customs and vocabulary can vary widely. Figure 3.3 summarizes beliefs and truths about French food.

Figure 3.3. Beliefs and Truths about French Food

Beliefs	*Truths*
• Drinks come with ice.	• Drinks come cooled, but not iced and it's often not even possible to get ice.
• Cafés serve hot food.	• Cafés generally don't serve any warm food, unless the sign says Brasserie as well.
• Breakfast includes meat such as bacon or sausage.	• Breakfast is a hot beverage and some sort of bread such as croissants.
• You can order just a dessert at a restaurant.	• Restaurants expect customers to order a full meal.
• A "salade" will contain lettuce.	• A "salade" will contain whatever is listed: a "salade de tomates" will be only sliced tomatoes.
• Salads come with French dressing.	• French salads come with a vinegar and oil dressing.

Geographical Gourmets

After research on a region or a country, have students develop a theory on how the particular geography, climate, and/or history of the region has influenced its architecture, its clothing, its language, and especially its cooking. Have each student or group find an authentic recipe from this country, prepare it, and bring it to class, explaining its history and the culture it comes from (and why it is authentic/typical). If possible, invite guests for the positive PR of an event like this.

Holidays

1. Go to a local grocery or convenience store and ask them for plain brown paper bags.

2. Have students research holiday customs for the target language, write a few sentences about each, and decorate the bags. (I preview what they write to avoid any embarrassing errors.)

3. Then return the bags to the stores for use during the holiday season. It's an excellent public relations project and gets a lot of good reactions from the community., Students do a terrific job, because they know their work will be on display.

Literature

For beginners, children's stories are a good place to start. There are many to be found at http://www.boowakwala.com, a web site in English, French, Spanish, Italian, and Dutch/Afrikaans. Don't forget your public library for books in your target language. Poetry is good, too. (See the next activity.)

Found Poetry

1. After reading a short work of prose, have students select 9 to 12 phrases no longer than six words in length from it. They will list these on a piece of paper.

2. Then have them cut these apart and arrange them according to these instructions:

   - Use the phrases you've chosen to create a poem that is your interpretation of the literary work. Manipulate the phrases until the manner in which they have been combined expresses something that you want to say about the original literary work. Cut apart your phrases into strips, and let's begin. Some advice:

   - You do not need to use rhymes.

   - You can reorganize the phrases and you can repeat words or groups of words many times, but you may not change the order in which the words appear on the phrase strips.

   - You may not add words either, although you may eliminate them—in other words, all of the words in the poem must come from the original text.

3. When you are ready, copy the poem onto unlined paper and illustrate it in color.

I Remember Venn ...

Have students use Venn diagrams to compare and contrast two different works. Within each Venn, you can place reminders of what to look for: tone, word choice, setting, characterization, or whatever. This is an easy way to lead students to recognize similarities and differences in literary style among well-known authors within the target language from one or more historical periods or even within the same period.

This can also be a tool to prepare students for a discussion. If you would like them to compare several different authors, students could each be assigned different combinations of the works you wish them to discuss. For example, if there are four readings, one student could have A and B, another A and C, another A and D, another B and C, another B and D, another C and D: six different combinations and six different forms of input for the discussion. This works well, especially in AP classes.

Finally, here are some good teacher resources for teaching Spanish poetry:

♦ Antologia de poesia espanola—una coleccion de poesias espanolas

This site contains short biographies of various poets, along with the text of their poems (with line numbers and an analysis of syllabication included for many of them). Find it at http://www.ipfw.edu/cm1/jehle/web/poesia.htm.

♦ Versificacion: Reconocer estrofas

This site has some very nice practice exercises (with answer keys) that allow students to practice analyzing the rhyme scheme, type of rhyme, and versification of poetry in Spanish. Go to http://faculty.washington.edu/petersen/321/estrof1.htm.

Geography

Here are a few ideas to try, if you haven't already:

♦ When we do the topic of the verb "to go" with places in a typical city, I teach about a real city. (I use a city I lived in.) The students read a map of the city, and I show slides and part of a video dealing with that city. Then we compare it with our own, using a Venn diagram.

♦ Get a piece of opaque plastic (many fabric stores stock this) and draw the country or countries you want to study on it. Lay it out on the floor, add a few toy cars, and you can teach the major features of the area: cities, mountains, rivers, and also "go," "went," sequencing words (such as "first," then, "later"), and colors, if you color the map (What color is Peru?). Play Geography Twister, coming up with your own directions for volunteers, such as, Put your right hand on the lake with the highest elevation, the city that produces mustard, the capital of Bayern, and so on.

♦ Have students research a monument or a city, then take a piece of cardboard and draw, paste, and/or write information about different aspects of it on the cardboard. Then cut it into about 30 pieces and store these in a recloseable bag. Have students put them together and learn at the same time.

To help with cultural geographic research, try these Internet sites:

The CIA, for information about almost any country: http://www.cia.gov

Tourism Offices Worldwide Directory:http://www.towd.com/

CLNet, the Chicano and Latino Network: http://latino.sscnet.ucla.edu/

Information in French and in English on various countries: http://www.e-thologies.com

Perspectives

Perspectives, the third part of Cultures, doesn't have its own standard, as it is interwoven with the other two aspects, products and practices, but there are certain things you can do that will focus on this important aspect.

One is to look at *politics*. Here are some interesting web sites to begin:

http://www.gksoft.com/govt/en/

http://www.politicalresources.net/home.htm

http://www.electionworld.org/index.html

http://rulers.org/

Another is to examine *current events* (see Chapter 6 for more on this topic). Research the influence of a foreign culture on American or world society, history, architecture, arts, or science.

Still another way to consider perspective is to look for ways in which the target language's culture has interacted with and influenced our own. (See Chapter 4, Connections.)

A fourth way is to examine *social behaviors*, such as the following activity:

The Relativity Theory of Time

Different cultures have different perceptions of time. The video "A Year in Provence" has a running joke about the French concept of being on time, involving the word *normalement*, and the Spanish culture has a similar situation involving the word *mañana*.

Center a classroom discussion around this idea, using a video or a story as an example, if possible.

Most Spanish countries are "polychronistic," which essentially means that events begin when everyone gets there and wants to start, and end when everyone agrees it's over, a delightfully nonstressful pace, but a bit exasperating to people used to orderly time schedules

In France, where the trains are famed for running precisely on time (when they're not out on strike) a 24-hour time system is used for schedules. If a train is supposed to arrive at 21:45 but doesn't arrive until 21:48, it is late. However, when people tell time verbally, as in setting up a social event, they use the less precise ordinary time telling using *moins, et quart* and *et demie.* Therefore, if they say they'll be somewhere at ten *moins le quart* and get there ten minutes late, no one will be surprised or upset. And for dinner parties, there is generally a half-hour's leeway before people feel obligated to provide any explanation for their time of arrival.

Both are good cases of how a language can reveal the perspectives of the target language culture.

4

Standard 3: Connections

> ◆ Connect with Other Disciplines and Acquire Information
>
> - Standard 3.1: Students reinforce and further their knowledge of other disciplines through the foreign language.
>
> - Standard 3.2: Students acquire information and recognize the distinctive viewpoints that are only available through the foreign language and its cultures.

Making connections is one of the most important tasks for a foreign language educator because these connections make it easier for the brain to store the foreign language. Instead of creating a special "foreign language" section, the information can be stored in an area where storage has already been implemented. The more pathways that are established to an item, the easier it is for the student's brain to retrieve the information.

Additionally, foreign languages are now required to show their relevance to curriculum in an educational system that must measure itself by reading and math scores on required, high-stakes tests. So, if we aren't thinking about these subject areas and consciously addressing them in our classrooms, foreign language classes run a risk of being considered irrelevant or, even worse, dispensable. We know this is not true, and, luckily, research is beginning to support us, especially in regards to the positive effect of language learning on test scores. Still, being able to document things we are doing towards interdisciplinary studies seems like a very good idea.

The fact is that learning a language or languages provides connections to additional bodies of knowledge that may be unavailable to someone who only speaks English. Connecting is a two-fold goal, as evidenced in Standard 3 of the national standards (or Standard 5 in the New York standards).

So, to implement this standard, we need to ask ourselves these questions:

- What opportunities do students have to access *authentic* information about other disciplines in the target language? Authentic instructional materials and realia are a key component in making those additional connections.

- What experiences do we arrange for our students that will help them make connections to other subject areas?

- What experiences do our students bring to our classroom that we can connect to the language we are teaching?

For one subject area, language arts (vocabulary and grammar) the overlap is immediately obvious and easy to make; in fact, Standard 4 (see Chapter 5) deals primarily with this connection between two languages and linguistic systems. For that reason, this chapter will deal primarily with connections to mathematics, science, social studies, and fine arts, as well as other fields.

Standard 3.1:
Other Disciplines

Students reinforce and further their knowledge of other disciplines through the foreign language.

Interdisciplinary learning is an important trend in education today. The idea is that learning should no longer be restricted to a specific discipline, and that teachers of foreign languages can and should make reference to and then build on the knowledge students acquire in other subject areas. In addition, students should leave our classes and be able to relate the information studied in their foreign language class to what they are learning in their other subjects. Thus, language instruction expands and deepens students' understanding of, and exposure to, other areas of knowledge, and new information and concepts from another class return to and are studied in the foreign language classroom.

This does not mean that we need to plan interdisciplinary units with all our students' other teachers. Start small: get together with the science teacher and see if you can teach your students some of the year's science vocabulary words as you do a unit on the rainforest, or see if the music teacher would consider having students sing a song in the target language. Have students use math skills in a discussion of the implementation of the new Euro currency. There are lots of connections out there to be made!

And remember, connections go *both ways:* your students will bring skills and information learned in other classes in to your classroom. Asking them to use the electronic research skills used in a computer basics class for an assignment in your class is a connection, too. All the reading, writing, and public speaking techniques from language arts are useful in your area, too—but it might be a very good idea to find out the expectations in those other classes, and make those carry over to your class as well. Your colleagues will thank you for doing this.

Figure 4.1 shows some connections that many of us do and which may be found in most texts.

Figure 4.1 Connections Between Other Subjects and Foreign Languages

Mathematics
- Beginning level: Numbers, adding, subtraction, multiplication and division. Telling time (24-hour method). Days of weeks and months. Metric measurements: prepare food using metric, convert temperature to Celsius, convert height and weight to meters and kilos.
- Intermediate: Currency conversions for shopping, converting prices on menus or salaries for various jobs, and so on.

Science
- Target language contributions to science: Famous scientists, centers for science study, products used in science from target language (TL) countries.
- Weather terms.
- Study of flora and fauna of TL regions.
- Discussions on ecological issues.
- Health unit: illnesses, vaccinations, medications.

Social Studies
- Geography: Study of countries that speak the TL. Learning geographical terms in the TL.
- History: Study history of TL countries. Influence of TL countries on our own history. Famous TL historical figures.
- Economics: economic bases of TL countries. The European Economic Community: what is it, and how does it work? The United Nations.
- Government: Governmental systems and leaders of TL nations.

Fine Arts
- Visual arts: Study famous artists and art styles originally from TL areas. Use basic elements of art: style, color, and content, to describe selected art works by TL artists.
- Music: Current and folk music and dances of TL countries (students both listen to and sing/perform), music history for TL regions, especially styles (for example, salsa) and instruments used (maracas, castanets).

(Figure continues on next page)

Language Arts	• Discuss rhetorical devices (simile, metaphor), rhyme and rhythm, genres (lyric or narrative), plot devices (foreshadowing, denouement), characterization (flat vs. round), and style (stream-of-consciousness).
	• Speech/broadcasting: Videotape presentations to send overseas or show to parents. (See Standard 2.3 Presentational mode, in Chapter 2.)
	• Writing techniques: Elements of composition, process-writing, textual analysis. Reading: Identify themes and main ideas, graphic organizers to keep track of information.
FACS (Family and Consumer Sciences, formerly Home Ec)	• Cooking: Typical TL foods, regional cooking styles, attitudes toward food, cooking utensils (molinilla, chopsticks), table manners, and the nutrition pyramid.
	• Concept of family in TL culture: Roles, child rearing practices, and so on.
	• Marriage: Typical age, attitudes, ceremonies, gifts.
	• Homes: Typical furnishings.
Physical Education	• Sports played in TL countries.
	• Athletes who speak the TL who play in our country.
Business	• Computer technology: Use of TL on the Internet. TL web sites. Exchange e-mail with keypals in TL country, make PowerPoints, use word processing software (including accent marks), chart survey results using Excel, use electronic research skills (upper levels even use TL Internet search engines) for research.
	• Business practices: Important international companies from TL countries and companies from here that operate branches in TL countries.
	• Marketing: Strategies used to market foreign products here, or our products overseas (ads, product adaptations).
	• Careers that use foreign languages as a job skill.

Generally, the above topics can be done at any level, with these differences:

♦ **Beginner level:** Primary focus on vocabulary, naming and identifying objects and people.

♦ **Intermediate level:** Basic discussion of subjects such as geography, mathematical problems, or history in sentence form. Listening to and/or viewing authentic conversations or discussions of these topics, such as a simple video on science in the target language. Reading short articles. Writing speeches or reports for other classes on information learned in foreign language class.

♦ **Advanced level:** Presenting reports in the target language orally and/or in writing on topics being studied in other classes. Writing reports for other classes using sources written in the target language. Discussion of topics from other school subjects or the workplace that include subjects such as politics, current events, worldwide health issues, and environmental concerns.

Those of us who are doing the above are already implementing Standard 3 in our classrooms. Making connections is what all seasoned teachers are skilled at. But, just in case you're thinking about adding a little more, here are some units you may wish to add or adapt for use in your classroom.

Webbing Ideas

Thematic webbing is not a new idea, but it is very important to do when planning an integrated cross-disciplinary unit. For this idea, which I got from Curtain and Pesola's wonderful book on teaching languages to children, the teacher chooses a word or an idea (or a book or story) as the central focus, and "spins" a web around that center with ideas from the various content areas. The web is a graphic representation of the unit. They also suggest involving students in this web-spinning process. Figure 4.2 is an example of an uncomplicated web.

**Figure 4.2. Choose a Color
(Based upon Curtain & Pesola, 1988)**

Purple

Music	Science	Language Arts	Math	Social Studies	Art	Health
Sing a song that includes the color purple	Add red and blue food coloring on the overhead to make purple.	Draw a red preposition (French à) and a blue article (le) combining to form au. Read, write or tell a story that uses the color purple.	Declare "purple day" and have students wear as many purple articles as possible. First count everything, and then divide by types of items. Make a chart or graph.	Look at flags that contain purple and locate those countries on the globe.	Find purple's complementary color on the color wheel and paint a picture using only those colors. Draw a picture to illustrate the story or song. Look at famous works of art that feature the color purple.	Find foods that are purple, and put them in appropriate food groups. Jump rope to a chant that uses the TL word for purple.

Okay with Hockey

A more complicated web might use a story at the center, such as one I do using the Canadian story, *Le Chandail,* about a boy who wanted a new hockey shirt.

1. Introduce the sports vocabulary (PE connection): using a handout of a hockey player, label all the equipment worn and used. On a handout of a hockey rink, label the various parts of the rink, and the types of players. Learn the basic rules for hockey (and watch part of a video of a game, describing it in the TL).

2. Have everyone wear a shirt for his or her favorite sport (including hockey). Do some math, sorting shirts by types of sports, colors, and so on.

3. Take students to a hockey web site and have each pick a team. Learn about the history of the city the team is from, and be able to explain the team's name and symbol and how those reflect the city's history.

4. Invent a name and a symbol for an imaginary hockey team from a city near here (art).

5. Learn about the physics of hockey, and how ice is made (science).

6. Read the story. (We listen to a tape of it as we read.)

7. Write a story about a similar incident in your own life.

8. Discuss poverty and rural life, and how those are important to the story.

The Sun is Shining Over Yonder

Language: Any
Level: Beginning to Intermediate
Connections: science, math, art, geography

1. Have students check out http://www.wunderground.com, where they'll be able to find what the weather is like in specific cities in TL countries and pull up the forecast in pretty much any language from Basque to Yiddish.

2. Assign them different TL countries, cities or regions (geography connection), and have them report on the day's weather, making a poster to go with their report. In addition to the standard greetings and farewells, a weather report generally tells

    • The day's weather so far

    • Future weather (evening and the following day)

    • The temperature (in Celsius—math connection—and in Fahrenheit)

4. Have students tell what they will wear, based upon the weather, or tell a bit about the city they are reporting from.

At Home with Art

Language: almost any

Connections: fine arts (architecture, photography), technology, speech

Level: if done in English, Beginning to Intermediate; in the target language, Advanced

This is a two-part lesson that also strongly incorporates Standard 6: Communities, and could lead to some newspaper coverage of your students' efforts, or at least some good public relations for your program in your school and your community.

1. Assign a report: To individual students or groups, assign a brief report on as many of the following architectural styles as may easily be found in countries that speak the target language:

   - Greek (Ionic, Doric, Corinthian)
   - Roman
   - Byzantine
   - Romanesque
   - Gothic
   - Neoclassical
   - Palladian
   - Baroque
   - Rococo
   - Georgian
   - Art Deco
   - Art Nouveau
   - Spanish Mission
   - Oriental
   - de Stijl
   - Bauhaus

   The report should include the following:

   - A description of the basic elements of the style and its place in history (time period it was popular, names associated with it, and so on.)

   - Specific information about the typical elements: roofs, arches, doorways, and windows, with a list of applicable terms (for example, Mansard roof, oriel, façade) to be given to students during the presentation

   - Visual examples of these elements from a TL country

   Because the technology for doing PowerPoint presentations is easily accessible where I teach, I generally make this report take the form of a PowerPoint at least seven slides long.

2. After a week's research, my student groups give their reports, one per day, with students taking notes, especially on the specifics of each style.

3. When the reports are concluded, each group is then given one more week's time to locate local examples of any of the architectural features discussed in class, returning on a specified date with at least five photos as well as the address each is to be found at. (We use the school's digital cameras.) Suggest that they investigate banks or other prominent businesses, churches, older houses, college

campuses, monuments, museums, and other similar structures. (Our town is small and rural. The requirement of five photos can be adjusted up or down depending on your own perception of how easily students will be able to locate these architectural elements.)

4. On the appointed day, have students display their finds, with the class identifying the style of each. (The students who discovered them may only drop hints if the class doesn't immediately see what they did.) The group then adds a colored marker (straight pin or push pin, a different color for each different architectural style found) to a map of the city or region.

5. Print out the better photo examples, and mount them, linked by yarn or string to the appropriate push pin on the map, in one of the school's main display cases for a memorable exhibit of your area's architectural riches (and your students' prowess in locating and identifying them).

Butterflies Are Free …

Language: Spanish

Connections: science, geography, art, language arts, fine arts

Levels: activities for all levels, but especially delightful with FLES students

The annual monarch butterfly migration to Mexico is a wonderful opportunity for Spanish classes to make connections with many different disciplines. To acquaint yourself with the basics about this migration before you begin this unit with students, visit the web site (in English) at http://www.monarchwatch.org/.

You might also wish to look at the Texas Parks & Wildlife Department sites at http://www.tpwd.state.tx.us/nature/research/monmig.htm and http://www.tpwd.state.tx.us/nature/education/tracker/monarch/index.htm. You could write a web search for your students using these sites. However, in the next section, there is an excellent web site that is in Spanish which you may prefer.

If you wish to add Standard 6: Communities to this lesson, at the Monarch Watch web site, you may sign your class up to participate in Monarch Watch's Adopt-a-School program, which accepts donations of money and school supplies for schools within the Monarch Reserve in Mexico. See http://www.monarchwatch.org/conserve/adopt.htm.

To raise money for this, and publicize this unit you are teaching, you might wish to make and raffle off paper monarch butterflies, folded in half, with the owner of a butterfly with a special color or marking inside it winning a special prize.

♦ Science, Geography, and Art Connections

1. With students, go to http://www.learner.org/jnorth for a great monarch migration activity. It is online all year and can be done in Spanish. From August to October on this site each year, thousands of American and Canadian students follow the migration of the monarch butterflies to Mexico. They also make and send paper butterflies, with notes written on them, to students living in the reserve areas in Mexico. The Mexican students "care for" these butterflies and, in the spring, send some back. (Usually, you'll receive butterflies from another school, and not your own, back.) You can also check this site for weekly updates on the migration most of the school year. This project is sponsored by UPS and the Annenberg Science Foundation.

2. Follow the photographic story of a school from Minnesota that visited the Monarch Butterfly sanctuary in Mexico. There are songs to listen to online and links to diagrams and further information on the life cycle of a butterfly available as your students follow the journey at http://www.sci.mus.mn.us/sln/monarchs/story/story.html.

3. In February, return to the web site "Spring's Journey North" at http://www.learner.org/jnorth/current.html. As the monarchs migrate north from February to June, schools throughout Mexico and the United States write in to report sightings, and the journey is plotted on maps that you can order for your students. The profiles of Mexican schools and the photos of the arrival of the monarchs can be very educating and exciting, all year!

4. Try the site at http://www.virtualmuseum.ca/Exhibitions/Butterflies/espanol/index.html, in Spanish, all about butterflies.

♦ Language Arts and Fine Arts Connections

1. The Putumayo Presents series has a CD of children's songs called *Volume 1: World Playground* that includes, among many different animal songs, a dance, "The Butterfly" by Colibri. Have your students listen to this, and dance or walk like a mariposa.

2. García Lorca wrote a children's poem called "La Mariposa." It's quite short and easy to read and/or memorize. In the poem, a child talks to a butterfly, asking it to stop fluttering and land somewhere. Go to http://www.poesia-infantil.com/lorca.html.

3. Here is a kinetic activity that incorporates art, music, and dance.

- Have students make butterflies from different colors of felt decorated with glitter and/or sequins. Attach each to an inexpensive mitten or glove (a good use for your school's Lost and Found "orphan" items).

- Ten children may participate at one time. Have them stand in a row, wearing their butterfly mittens or gloves on a hand tucked behind their backs, and sing the following song to the tune of "Ten Little Indians":

  > Uno y dos y tres mariposas
  > Cuatro y cinco y seis mariposas
  > Siete y ocho y nueve mariposas
  > Diez mariposas son.

- As each number is sung, a new student's butterfly will "flutter" out from behind his/her back, and dance around, until all ten are fluttering. Then sing it backward. (Older children can do this, but with younger ones, you'll have to do it for them.):

  > Diez y nueve y ocho mariposas
  > Siete y seis y cinco mariposas
  > Cuatro y dos y tres mariposas,
  > Una mariposa es.

A more active variation on the above song that visually reenacts the migration is to label one side of the room USA and the opposite wall Mexico. The ten students would start lined up along the USA wall and their butterflies would "migrate" to the opposite wall, and, during the singing of the second portion, they would return to the United States from Mexico. This would be really cute to do for a school assembly or videotape for parent conferences.

Souvenirs, Souvenirs ...

Languages: All

Level: Beginning

Connections: Geography, art (design), mathematics (currency conversion), business (marketing a shirt)

1. Have students research a country, a region, or a city that speaks the target language, just for information on location, monuments, and other items relating to tourism, including currency exchange rates (see web sites later).

2. Have them design (and make, if the art teacher will help with silk-screening) a "souvenir" tee-shirt for this place.

3. Have them, as part of a report, show the location for this place on a map and tell a little about its geography (mountains/hills/plains, rivers or oceans, and so on). Also have them model their shirt and explain the items they put on it, plus the price they "paid" for it and what that would be in American money. You can also have them describe two or three other souvenirs (items typical of that place) that they purchased, along with prices paid.

4. It is even possible, if other students are interested in a particularly attractive shirt, to consider selling a student's design as a project for your language club. With the help of a business teacher, have students price blank tee-shirts and other materials needed to make the shirt, figure a profit percentage, take orders and collect money, develop a work schedule for producing the shirts, and deliver or market them.

A Bicycle Built for Two ... or More

Languages: French, German, Italian, Spanish

Levels: Intermediate to Advanced

Connections: Geography, history, physical education, math

For years, in Europe, champion bicycle racers have been national heroes. With the recent successes of Lance Armstrong, bicycle racing has captured our attention here in the United States, and we can better appreciate the admiration of other countries for their talented riders. The U.S. Postal Service team has been very successful, and we derive great pride from this. Take advantage of this to stimulate students' interest in geography, history, and fitness.

There is a major race that we can use for almost any TL unit on sports. The Giro d'Italia takes place in late May, early June; the Tour de France in July; and the Vuelta a España in September. There is also a Tour of Germany in late May to early June, a new addition only three years old but fast becoming popular.

1. Start with the vocabulary. With students, brainstorm necessary words: race, lap, rest, climb, wind, cap, water bottle, pedal, time trial, and so on. Have groups make posters: a cyclist, a bicycle, and a typical day's schedule (use the Internet as a resource for what a typical schedule looks like), all labeled in the TL. Make sure they know enough vocabulary to adequately describe a race, or to watch one as it is televised in the TL. To check, have them write a version of the "Tortoise and the Hare" fable, using different animals!

2. For whatever cycling tour is in your TL, get the planned itinerary. Assign other student groups to research the major cities along the route: terrain (will this be an easy day of riding?), local history and sights to see (what might they ride past?): geography/history connection.

3. Use the route, and calculate distances by changing kilometers into miles. Do the same with the heights of various mountain passes the race goes through (math connection).

4. Give each student group a particular rider to cheer for, and have them research that person's team, personal achievements, training regimen (exercises, diet, and so on), writing a short report that ends with their guess what place he will finish in: PE connection.

5. Also have them make up cheers to shout as he rides past, and a message to paint onto the road for him to read. Give prizes for the best effort. Have student go online to send messages of support to their riders; you won't believe the excitement when they (occasionally) get an answer.

6. If possible, show a videotape of the previous year's race. (ESPN 2 is a good resource as they broadcast all four of the races listed.) Another possibility is to have a tricycle race, or a foot race. (We did one, flipping a crepe as they ran.) Make sure the spectators cheer for their favorites and put their new TL vocabulary to work!

Standard 3.2:
Acquire Information

Students acquire information and recognize the distinctive viewpoints that are only available through the foreign language and its cultures.

This portion of the standard emphasizes what I generally call the "new window on the world" they have opened as a consequence of their learning a new language. From the first levels of language learning, students can begin to examine a variety of sources intended for native speakers (for example, newspaper headlines), and extract information. As they become more proficient in the language, they can begin to seek out materials of interest to them, analyze the content, compare it to information available in their own language, and assess the linguistic and cultural differences. This is especially striking in two areas: holidays, and current events.

Fat Tuesday Fun

Languages: European

Levels: Any

Connections: Art (masks), FACS (food), technology (research)

Mardi Gras is one of the holidays that lend themselves to "compare and contrast" because it cross-culturally spans several languages and countries. I've celebrated Mardi Gras in France as well as in the United States, in Germany (Fasching), in Italy (Carnevale), and have seen web sites for other celebrations on every continent.

This is a great chance for your school's different foreign language classes or clubs to find some common ground. Have your students research how this holiday is celebrated by those who speak the TL, then meet with and exchange the results of their research with the other language classes that meet during the same time slot, or with any other interested classes. (Social studies or FACS would be obvious connections.)

Because Mardi Gras is a time for disguises and elaborate costumes, have classes compete to make the most beautiful masks. We begin with a plain paper plate, adding elastic to turn it into a mask, and adding yarn, buttons, crepe paper, construction paper, beads, sequins, glitter, feathers—whatever you can get the students to bring in. I take group pictures every year and post them on my web site for students to view and show their families. I've even gotten comments from web-surfing strangers from overseas that those were their favorite part of my site.

An interdisciplinary cook-off with a coinciding language and/or foods class would be fun, as well, with each group presenting the traditional TL food for this holiday. As a starting point, I recommend http://www.holidays.net/mardigras/index.htm and http://www.howstuffworks.com/mardi-gras.htm. There are quite a few good web searches to be found at Trackstar at http://trackstar.hprtec.org. (Search for Mardi Gras or what this holiday is called in your TL.)

In Louisiana, participants get Mardi Gras beads or doubloons, which are easy to order from many sources (online or catalogs such as Oriental Trading Company). The doubloons often have historical information on them: Greek mythology, famous rulers or battles, and so on, and these can also become a small learning opportunity.

Finally, how about a little friendly competition? We have a short "around the world" (around the room) race in which volunteer students carry small (cold) frying pans containing "racing crepes" that they must flip every third step of the way. No penalty for dropping these, but it does slow the person down. I saw this race in London one year during this holiday. I have a short video of it taken from CNN and have read reports of similar races in France, so it is authentic.

The connections and comparisons this will give rise to should be obvious.

Where in the World Is ...

Languages: Any but best results are, I think, with Spanish or French

Levels: Intermediate

Connections: Geography, computer skills, careers class

I think we've all heard the "when am I ever going to have to use this" whine before. Here is a good short lesson to answer that complaint, along with providing a little career-oriented information.

1. Provide students with two different colored crayons or markers, and a world map. Have them color all areas that speak the TL in one color, and all English-speaking areas in the other; in bilingual cases like Canada, they may want to draw stripes or polka dots or something. Give them about ten minutes or so.

2. Using a world map or an overhead, go continent by continent and locate the places they can go that would speak the TL. Students generally are quite unaware of even places that speak English (such as New Zealand).

3. Break students into groups, assign each a different TL region and, using the Internet if possible, look for reasons to visit each area (especially career-related ones)—American companies located there, and so on. Have them report one or two of their "most interesting" reasons for going there, and two careers that might take them there, to the group. Suggested web sites are www.monster.com for careers, and any good search engine (I'm partial to www.google.com).

My purpose in this unit, in addition to providing some career guidance information, is to encourage students to view TL areas of the world as interesting possibilities in their futures, and to underline the global economic community that we are a part of.

Comparing Currents

Languages: Any

Level: Advanced

Connections: Social studies (history, economics, current events)

This simple, short two-day lesson may really open some new cultural perspectives for your students.

1. Give students a current events topic of your choice, from here in the United States. Here are some examples:

The death penalty (an execution)	A terrorist act
A controversial lawsuit	An election
A school sporting event	A military issue or action
A labor issue such as a strike	An educational reform proposal
A wedding or divorce	

2. Using the Internet, have students search for an equivalent article in the TL, not about the same event, but a similar one in a TL area. (Yahoo has current events in almost every country.)

3. With a Venn diagram (interlocking circles), have them list the main points of each story. If, for example, the left circle is the U.S. story, any unique points of that story would be in the U.S. circle only, but if there are things in common between both stories, those would be listed in the area where the two circles overlap. Then the right hand circle would be used for the TL article, with the same procedure.

4. The above topics should lead students to learn about how the TL country's political, educational, social or legal systems, and attitudes and enthusiasms are like or unlike our own. On Day 2 of this lesson, have students present their topic and conclusions and resulting impressions or opinions. Discussion is generally a result of these topics. Allow students to follow up these discussions for more information (for example, whether military service is optional in the TL country, and at what age it is usually done, why other countries

do or don't have the death penalty, how old you must be to drink/marry/quit school, and so on).

Go Right to the Source

Languages: Any

Level: Intermediate

Connections: almost anything!

The key to reaching the goals of Standard 3.2 is to have current, authentic input for your students. Get multiple copies of a TL newspaper, magazine, or TV Guide. Give these to students and ask them to read them, extract examples on topics you've chosen, and present their impressions on the following:

- ♦ Popular trends: music, movie and/or TV programs

- ♦ Perceived beauty as depicted in magazines: weight, hairstyles and colors, clothing styles and colors, accessories, makeup and nails

- ♦ Celebrities in TL culture

- ♦ Characteristics of a model citizen (husband/wife/mother/father) as well as typical forms of employment (and salaries)

- ♦ Typical homes and furnishings (including costs)

- ♦ Conventional foods eaten and prepared (brand names and costs, if possible)

- ♦ If materials are age-appropriate, adolescent values and behaviors (what should one own, wear, be interested in?)

A logical follow-up to this is to have students write and film their own commercial or newscast on the topic investigated that would show what their conclusions were about the TL culture as revealed in the print media.

If I Ran This School …

Language: Any

Level: This would require the subjunctive, so Intermediate to Advanced

Connections: Students' own experiences and beliefs

1. Provide students with information on the TL culture's schools. (Most texts do a fairly good job with this, though having keypals—penpals via Internet—with students in a TL country would be a wonderful resource as well.) Tell them they will be exchange students, and ask them what they will want to know about their new school before they go there. List all the things they wish to know on the board or an overhead.

2. Then, use their list, and ask them to write a short essay in which they create a plan for a model school based on the best points of our educational system and theirs. Your plan should include all the points of information you see listed on the board, and if these are not included in that, list the following:

   - A description of the system (what age students would attend what school)

   - Typical course offerings for a student your age

   - A sample daily student schedule, showing the day from beginning to end, including breaks and meals

   - A description of the faculty (sexes, ages, educational backgrounds)

   - A public relations brochure for your school

   Everything must be done in the target language.

Finally, they say music is the "international language." I do know that you can find out a lot about a country by listening to its music:

Music Video Project

Languages: Any

Connections: Music department, art, broadcasting class

Level: Advanced

As we learn to appreciate the music of the target culture, students are usually drawn to several favorite songs. Assign one of those songs to a student and pair them with a student from the art department and the video production class for the following project:

1. Group students, one from each class. The language student should choose a musical piece, and explain it to the art and broadcasting student.

2. The art student will begin to prepare a storyboard of the images to be used in shooting the video, with input from the group.

3. The video student will add notes on camera and filter needs, angles, special effects, and so on to prepare a sort of script for shooting the video.

4. Make the storyboard the first item due. Examine those with students, and give feedback and suggestions.

5. The script should be the next piece handed in. After approval of the storyboard and script, shooting may begin.

6. After shooting is complete, give a final deadline for completion of all editing, and schedule a party for viewing the videos.

Figure 4.3 shows the product descriptor and the rubric for this project.

Figure 4.3. Music Video Product Descriptor and Rubric

Several things about the video will be important in determining the grade for this project.

- ◆ Quality of the imagery
  - The images shown should correspond to the words in the song, and be shown at the exact time those words are heard.
  - Images used should be easy to see (clear and in focus).
  - The flow of images should be fluid, with no blank spots.

- ◆ Quality of the music
  - Music should be an essential part of the video, and not just background for the images.
  - The music should be heard continually and without pauses.
  - The entire song should be in the video, with no part left out.
  - The music should be easy to hear, and the words clear.

- ◆ Introduction and conclusion of video
  - The beginning should include the title of the song and the name of the performer.
  - The end should contain the name(s) of the people working on this project.

- ◆ Translation (if used)
  - Translation should be as faithful as possible to the original.
  - It should be read in time with the music.

- ◆ Different scenes
  - Each different scene should illustrate an image in the song.
  - It should be easy to tell why this scene/image was chosen to complement the song.
  - At least one of the images in the video should be a work of art.

- ◆ Project Rubric

25 points	Punctuality Attendance Cooperation in group
25 points	Choice of music Fitting music to visual images
10 points	Storyboard
40 points	Technical elements: • Edits (cuts and dissolves) • Graphics (words at beginning and end) • Audio quality

5
Standard 4: Comparisons

> ◆ Develop Insight into the Nature of Language and Culture
>
> • Standard 4.1: Students demonstrate understanding of the nature of language through comparisons of the language studied and their own.
>
> • Standard 4.2: Students demonstrate understanding of the concept of culture through comparisons of the cultures studied and their own.

This standard (which seems to be similar to New York's Standard 6) is the one of the five for which, in my opinion, there are the fewest resources available for teachers' and students' use. In brief, few texts contain strategies or suggestions for this standard, surprisingly, and so it must be consciously implemented.

To use this standard in any classroom, the key is to give students opportunities (and incentives) to analyze and compare the many linguistic and cultural features of their native and target language environments. Students who have good study skills instinctively seek out patterns in a language and compare them to their own, but many need to be taught how to do this and helped to recognize the similarities and differences; this is where the "incentives" part of the application becomes important.

Therefore, in this chapter, you will find some ideas on strategies to help students make these comparisons and contrasts, in addition to the lesson and unit suggestions as in previous chapters.

Standard 4.1:
Comparing languages

Students demonstrate understanding of the nature of language through comparisons of the language studied and their own.

In this portion of Standard 4, students are asked to examine the target language and English and draw conclusions or develop hypotheses about structure and usage of these languages. Being proficient at this will benefit them both in the TL, where learning will become easier as they learn to analyze new situations and apply previously learned skills and observations, and in their native language, where they may apply the knowledge acquired in the language classroom (especially the grammatical knowledge) to better understand English structures. Thus, learning a foreign language both enhances and reinforces the grammar learned in the language arts class. And this can be done from Day One of the first language class, and continued as different elements are presented.

Some basic concepts important to this standard are described here:

♦ Languages borrow words and phrases from one another (but sometimes change the spelling: *futbol*, Spanish; *rosbif*, French). Teach your students to look for cognates (related words). I make a point of doing this as it makes them relate English to new vocabulary. For example, when we hit *mort* (dead) I ask them to think of English words, and they come up with mortuary, mortician, mortal, and immortal. And they remember that word from then on.

♦ Some idiomatic expressions or vocabulary words cannot be translated well from one to another but are important to use for good communication. An example would be expressions that use *hacer* (Spanish) and *avoir* (French).

♦ Word order may differ in another language (for example, adjective placement).

♦ Tone of voice, volume, pitch, and gestures are as much a part of a language as the vocabulary.

And now for a few lessons that implement aspects of Standard 4.

The Borrowers

Level: Beginner

Language: French, but easily adaptable to any language

1. On the very first day of my Level 1 classes, I assign students to bring back, the next day, eight French words or phrases that we use in English. They may consult a dictionary, another teacher, a parent, or a friend for help. I give them a bit of guidance as we talk about words that use accents as a characteristic of French, as well as common endings like -age.

2. The next day, we graffiti these onto a big piece of paper and discuss them ("How many of these are political/legal/food/fine arts terms?"), following up with a handout with more difficult phrases such as *savoir faire* and *coup d'état*. This makes them instantly aware that our language has many words borrowed from the target language.

3. It is also a valuable way of helping students see that the spelling of a word in the TL and its pronunciation has both similarities to and differences from our own language. Usually the first day, we focus on the [a] and [i] sounds and their spellings, as English usually keeps the French pronunciation when it "adopts" a word. (For example, compare/contrast the pronunciation of the *i* in China and in machine. French words keep the "ee" sound for the "i" spelling. So do Spanish ones.)

4. Other good follow-up activities:

    Looking at a state map for cities, rivers, mountains and other features with French (Spanish, German, Latin) names. (Most texts do this sort of thing for the entire nation, but I think doing just your state, places your students are likely to travel, is much more meaningful and likely to "stick" or even come up in conversation during a family trip, for example.) Because beginning students rarely can recognize these unaided, I've had student aides draw a state map with only French-named features on it, that we look at, pronounce, and discuss possible reasons for its having that name—for example, Terre Haute means, and is located on, high ground.

    Giving students (as good pronunciation practice!) a list of words the TL has borrowed from English, to show that the borrowing goes both ways.

Strategy 1: Concept Deduction

This teaching strategy forces students to look for patterns in a language; and because those patterns must be located before comparisons can be made, it is an important one to use. You won't have to teach the actual concept in English, or use grammatical terms; students will discover, like Sherlock Holmes, that the power of deduction will lead them to knowledge.

First, students must be presented with raw data (sentences or phrases in the TL). These may be from an authentic source or generated by the teacher. It is best if they are similar in every way except for the variations you wish the students to focus on, for example, that they all have pronoun subjects, or noun subjects, so that this does not detract from the features you wish them to notice.

Then, have students complete a sort of graphic organizer that asks them to develop a theory ("How is this verb tense formed?") or locate and fill in the most important characteristics of the selection ("What sorts of things is the imperfect tense being used to describe?" "What types of verbs are used in this paragraph?").

Then, students should test their theory, refining it if necessary, with further examples, and then be asked to display their conclusions by generating their own examples.

This is an excellent method to use with grammar as it leaves students ready for a discussion of the time or tense's characteristics and those of its English equivalent(s). Here, however, is a more stylistically oriented example of this method, based upon authentic materials:

A Nose for News

Languages: Any

Level: Intermediate to Advanced

This unit is most effectively done if it is possible to obtain a video tape of a newscast in the target language, although it is perfectly adaptable (and perhaps easier for students) to achieve the same results with articles taken from a newspaper.

1. Show students a newscast in the target language, and have them complete the graphic organizer shown in Figure 5.1.

2. Then assign them to watch a newscast in English, and fill out the other half of the organizer.

3. The next day, during a discussion, fill out the same form on the overhead projector based on your students' observations. Divide them into groups, and assign a brief news broadcast in the target language, using elements from the target language side of the organizer.

Figure 5.1. News Broadcast Form

	Target Language Broadcast	*English Language*
Basics: • How many presenters? • Male or female? • Did they name their name(s)? • Setting: furniture, background		
Introduction: • How did they greet the viewers? • Which form of "you" was used, if any? • Other opening remarks:		
First story: • Topic: • Verb tense(s) used: • Visuals?		
How many news items were covered? How many "people profile" stories?		
Weather: • Location of weather segment in broadcast: beginning? middle? end? • What similarities to ours? • Differences?		
Sports: • Types of sports reported on: • Location of sports segment in broadcast: beginning? middle? end?		
Ending: • Final topic discussed: • Closing comments:		
Miscellaneous: • Were news items grouped in any way, such as regional/national/international? • Were they the same types of items you would see here? • What were the differences, if any?		

Strategy 2: Memory Model

Memory Model is a simple way for students to relate new vocabulary to previously learned material (Standard 3) and English structures and vocabulary. For words they are having trouble remembering, encourage students to make up a story. The story must

- use the vocabulary word twice, once in the target language, and once in English.

- be creative—the weirder, sillier, grosser, gorier, or wittier the better.

  Creativity encourages students to explore how the target language word looks (reminding them of an English word that looks similar) or sounds (reminding them of an English word that sounds similar). Otherwise, they will come up with a story that simply replaces the English equivalent with the target language word, over and over.

- have a visual (drawn in color) to go with it, which does *not* have the word on it.

After students have gotten their stories and drawn the visuals, have them share the stories with each other by telling the story while pointing out various features of the drawing. These are usually quite entertaining and even sometimes impressively creative.

Then, leave the drawings up in the classroom and have students refer to them; tell the stories to a partner, practice telling themselves the stories, and so on, until the difficult vocabulary is learned.

A French example: for the word *balayer* (to sweep) the students notice its visual (and sound) similarity to *ballet* and the -er ending that usually signifies a person who does something, in English, and draw a ballerina with a broom, sweeping. What they are sweeping is sometimes gory, sometimes very silly … always memorable.

A final, very important step in comparing and contrasting the target language and English would be to have the more advanced classes discuss the strengths and limitations of each language. Now, when so many students have access to online translators, many teachers are pulling their hair out over the poor results for those who use these. Figure 5.2 (pp. 99–103) displays a wonderful project that not only points out these aspects of the language but also, at the same time, clearly shows students the strengths and limitations of the translation programs available.

(Text continues on page 104.)

Figure 5.2. Computer-Assisted Translation Project

In this project, you will

1. Locate and use computerized language translation tools.

   You may want to try "Free Online Translation Systems" web page located at http://www.word2word.com/free.html, or EL Easton's Multilingual Online translators at http://eleaston.com/lgs-dict.html#tran.

2. Evaluate the quality of said translation tools.

3. Consider the ethical ramifications for the proper use of translation tools.

Date due: _____, when the bell finishes ringing to signal the beginning of class.

Format: Typed and in a folder with brads/rings. *No pockets*

Penalties: –15 points if handed in the same day, after the bell

            –25 per calendar day if later

The world is changing. Technology that was unimaginable 25 years ago is commonly available today. One of these new technologies is computer-assisted translation. Often we see a new technology and accept it without evaluating it. But is it good in all situations? Is it ethical? Is it wise? When is it a useful tool, and when does it cause more problems?

♦ When you are a professional, in which circumstances will you require a professional translation, and when is online translation acceptable?

This exercise will help you evaluate computer-assisted translations. You will complete a project with all the following items printed out and either stapled together or in a folder:

♦ **Research:** Locate and use computerized language translation tools

   A. Locate at least five Internet translation services. List them (name and URL) in your project.

   B. Try to find a non-Internet product. (Note: Ask family and friends if they have one. Do not buy any product.)

   C. Translate the following pairs of sentences on each of the five Internet translation services and also on the non-Internet product:

1. The *bats fly* into the room.
2. The *bats fly* into space when the *batters* hit too hard.
3. The best cake *batter* has sugar and cinnamon in it.
4. I like ice cream with *nuts*
5. My father buys *nuts* and bolts at the *hardware* store.
6. I often buy new *hardware* and software for my computer.
7. I *can* sing.
8. I have a *can* of Coke.
9. *Can* you dance the *can-can*?
10. When I was a *kid,* I *found* a silver dollar.
11. On what date did Bill Gates *found* Microsoft?
12. The *kid* and the nanny goat ran in the fields and ate the flowers.
13. My father doesn't like *to fly*.
14. The *fly* was *flying* around my head.
15. The *fly* on his jeans was broken.

D. Analyze the way the various programs handled the homonyms in the previous section. Look up the homonyms in a dictionary to be certain which word is correct in each sentence.

E. Write a one-paragraph autobiography in English. Put it in your project.

F. Enter the one-paragraph autobiography in each of the five Internet translators and also in the non-Internet product. Translate your autobiography to Spanish. Print out and include in your project.

G. Write a one-paragraph autobiography in Spanish. Put it in your project.

H. Enter the Spanish paragraph in each of the five Internet translators and also in the non-Internet product. Translate your autobiography to English. Print out each one and put them in the project.

I. Choose the *best* of the translators. Enter your English paragraph; translate it to Spanish. Translate the Spanish to French. Translate the French to English. Print out each translation (Eng-Sp-Fr-Eng) and include it in your project. Compare the first English to the final English.

J. Copy a paragraph of text written originally in Spanish: you may take something from the newspaper, a children's book you find online, and so on. Feed it into the best of the translators and translate it into English. Enter both the Spanish and English in your project.

K. Ask a native speaker (preferably an ESL student) to read the Spanish in every case. Ask if he or she understands the Spanish as it comes from the computer-assisted translator.

♦ **Analysis:** *Write* a short paper in which you analyze the proper and improper use of computer-assisted translators. *Analyze* each item in terms of practical, legal and ethical ramifications and *explain* what the legal and ethical considerations would be. What is the basis for your ethical considerations? When would it be wiser to pay a professional translator? Include the following (and any other uses you think of):

- Classroom exercises for which you will be graded
- Letters from family or friends who speak another language
- Classroom use to help a non-English-speaking student understand the lesson or classroom instructions
- A legal contract (preliminary version, to understand what it says)
- A legal contract (version that you sign, binding version)
- Any information (online or text) that you need for information you will be using in a research paper
- Instruction manual for non-English-speaking employees
- Safety manual for non-English-speaking employees
- Letter that the school sends home to Spanish-speaking parents
- Letter that the school sends home to Bulgarian-speaking parents
- Medical information from a doctor to patient
- Usage information from the pharmacist to the patient

♦ **Conclusions:** When is it acceptable, legal, ethical, and prudent to use a computer-assisted translation? When is it better to pay a professional translator? How will you be able to analyze the state of the art in 15 years? What will your profession be? What are the ramifications of this study for your field when you are 30 or 40 years old?

Rubric: Computer-Assisted Translation

♦ **Research:** 35 points

_____ Locate five Internet translation services. List them (name and URL).

_____ Try to find a non-Internet product. (Note: ask family and friends if they have one. Do not buy any product.)

_____ Write a paragraph analyzing the way the programs handled the homonyms. Look the homonyms up in a dictionary to be certain which use is correct.

_____ Write a one-paragraph autobiography in English. Put it in your project

_____ Enter the one-paragraph autobiography in each of the five Internet translators and also in the non-Internet product. Translate your autobiography to Spanish.

_____ Write a one-paragraph autobiography in Spanish. Put it in your project.

_____ Enter the Spanish paragraph in each of the five Internet translators and also in the non-Internet product. Translate your autobiography to English. Print out each one and put them in the project.

_____ Choose the best of the translators. Translate. Print out each translation (Eng-Sp-Fr-Eng) and include it in your project. Compare the first English to the final English. Analyze.

_____ Copy a paragraph of text written originally in Spanish. Translate to English and print. Enter both the Spanish and English in your project.

_____ Reaction of native speaker who reads the Spanish in every case. Include the name of the native speaker and his or her reaction.

♦ **Analysis:** 50 points

Paper: Analyze the proper and improper use of computer-assisted translators.

Analyze each item in terms of practical, legal and ethical ramifications and *explain* what the legal/ethical considerations would be.

What is the basis for your ethical considerations? Include the following (and any other uses you think of):

_____   Classroom exercises for which you will be graded

_____   Letters from family or friends who speak another language

_____   Classroom use to help a non-English-speaking student understand the lesson or classroom instructions

_____   A legal contract (preliminary version, to understand what it says)

_____   A legal contract (version that you sign, binding version)

_____   Any information (online or text) that you need for information you will be using in a research paper

_____   Instruction manual for non-English-speaking employees

_____   Safety manual for non-English-speaking employees

_____   Letter that the school sends home to Spanish-speaking parents

_____   Letter that the school sends home to Bulgarian-speaking parents

_____   Medical/pharmaceutical use

_____   School web site; Other

Conclusion: How good are machine translations? When should they be used? When you are a professional, how will you evaluate the state of the art and whether it should be used in your field?

♦ **Format:**

15 Points		*How to Lose Points*		
_____	Neatness	Late paper: _____		–15 same day
_____	Format		_____	–25 each calendar day late
_____	Typed			
_____	Rubric signed and included at the beginning of the project			
_____	Table of contents; page number on each page			

(Contributed by Carol Ross Stacy, of Newman Smith High School, Carrollton, Texas)

Standard 4.2:
Comparing Cultures

Students demonstrate understanding of the concept of culture through comparisons of the cultures studied and their own.

In this portion of Standard 4, students do the same thing they did in comparing and contrasting the two languages, but this time instead of languages, they look at practices, products, and perspectives (Standard 2) in the TL culture and look for similarities to and differences from their own culture. In doing this, they will also learn to hypothesize about cultural systems in general.

My own personal view of this activity is that most teenagers can immediately see the differences with little prompting from us. Perhaps middle-school students are best at this. They are hypercritical of anything that is out of the ordinary, and usually reject it. Therefore, I think that foreign language teachers should try hardest to help students find common ground between the target culture and their own. Instead of just showing students the wild, weird, and unusual, show them how many things they have in common with students whose native language is the target language. Doing this will tie in nicely with Standard 5: Communities, in which we endeavor to make students into good citizens. Tolerance and understanding of cultural differences is a big step toward that.

Strategy 3: Venn Diagrams

Venn diagrams (two interlocking circles) are a great strategy for achieving this goal. Start with an easy project like this one:

Calendar Illustrations

Language: Any

Level: Beginning

Give students a target language calendar, and a Venn diagram. The diagram is two interlocking circles, with the left one labeled "TL Calendar" and the right one labeled "American calendar." Instruct students that they must find at least 11 things to write down about the calendars; if the feature is unique to the TL calendar, they are to write it in the left circle; if unique to the American calendar, in the right circle; and any features that are common to both go in the center. I also tell them that they should have almost equal numbers of similarities as they have differences. (This usually stops them from writing things like, "The days are in TL, the month is in TL" and so on; instead they focus more on the structure.) To get 11 things, they are going to have to really look at the calendars.

Then discuss the differences first, and finish with the similarities.

Then talk about why people have calendars, and what calendars may show about their cultural attitudes. (For example, ask them for theories why theirs starts on Monday and ours on Sunday.)

Here are some other things to use Venn diagrams:

♦ Watch a video tape of television news, commercials, or weathercasts in the TL. Hopefully students will recognize that all cultures have symbols, music, and advertisements, and that all serve similar purposes.

♦ Watch a movie about holiday celebrations, for example, one on Christmas celebrated in a TL country. Other obvious comparisons would be of Halloween to Dia de los Muertos, or of Bastille Day to our Independence Day.

♦ Compare a Mother Goose rhyme in both languages.

♦ Compare two different regions of a country that speaks the TL.

♦ Read an essay on TL politics, their educational system, their environmental policy, or other cultural institutions (for example, welfare, taxes, laws).

♦ Look at a drawing of a typical house, table setting, class schedule, restaurant menu, or other artifact.

♦ Watch a video of people greeting each other, dating, playing sports, or other social activities, or working. Look for words, body language (gestures and how close they stand, whether they look into each other's eyes, and/or smile), tone of voice (and volume and pitch), as well as looking to see if males behave differently than females.

Venn diagrams don't have to be circles. I do hearts at Valentine's Day, or triangles, stars or whatever seems appropriate to the season or the activity.

Strategy 4: Performance

Simulations or actual performances are activities with very high retention of the material experienced. Arrange for students to purchase items at your "store," check into your "hotel," prepare and/or eat authentic foods, dance authentic dances, play a sport, or visit a museum and look at paintings or sculptures. Read aloud with appropriate intonation and pronunciation. Recite proverbs, short anecdotes, or poetry; put on a play. Throw a quinceañera or a traditional wedding ceremony and celebration.

The hands-on aspect will more firmly fix the material in their brains and at the same time, give them feedback as to how proficient they are at doing these things (and therefore whether they need to work harder to learn them or not).

A brief oral or written description of the experience (perhaps a journal entry?) will force students to think about and draw conclusions regarding the cultural aspect experienced. Too many times we provide experiences for our students, for example a food tasting, without asking them to process and reflect upon the experience.

In addition to the Venn diagram, don't forget the graphic organizer, for activities like the following:

To Live Life Fully

Have students go to the CIA countries web site at http://www.odci.gov/cia/publications/factbook/index.html and compare TL countries using a graphic organizer such as the one shown in Figure 5.3.

Figure 5.3. Graphic Organizer for To Live Life Fully

	USA	France	Canada	Senegal	Morocco	Haiti
Population						
Birth rate						
Death rate						
Religion(s)						
Literacy rate						
Government type						
Suffrage						
GDP per capita (avg. income)						
Population below poverty line						
Unemployment rate						

This can be a real eye-opener for some of them, and should definitely lead to some discussion and theories as to why the differences exist.

Let Your Fingers Do the Walking

I learned recently that, if a school requests foreign phone books, they can get them at no charge. Have your school secretary or treasurer (whoever orders such things) contact the telephone company and get you the Yellow Pages from a major target language city.

Then, let your creativity go. Just copy a page or two.

♦ Have beginning students read you the phone numbers of businesses you name, or tell you the name of a business whose number you read to them.

♦ Have intermediate students pick out the restaurant that sounds best to them, and tell why.

♦ Have intermediate students look at various store ads, and create a shopping experience skit to go with a particular store's advertised specialization.

♦ Have advanced students select a business they are interested in, and write them, asking about career opportunities or another topic of interest to them.

Strategy 5: Personalize!

We all love to learn more about and talk about ourselves. So, the best strategy for teaching culture is to help our students know themselves better. Instead of a constant focus on TL countries, turn the tables and focus on the here and now. Students will tune out the "this is how *they* do things," but if you focus on "how *we* do things" they perk up and pay attention.

Have them read an essay about what TL teens think we're like; seeing our culture through others' eyes (with what aspects they focus on, or think are weird or bad) is a high-interest activity. A variation on this is to have students read the article describing the weird cultural habits of the Nacirema at http://www.msu.edu/~jdowell/miner.html. Then tell them that Nacirema is "American," backward, and they've just read about themselves. Then discuss cultural stereotyping and its pitfalls.

Identify as many contributions as possible that the foreign culture has made to ours: foods, celebrations, and traditions. Do ones they'll really love, such as the following:

Chocolate!

Connections (Standard 3): History, science, fine arts, language arts, home economics

Levels: All

When everyone's spirits seem to need a lift, why not try the "Food of the Gods," as many web sites call it. I read somewhere that it takes most of the world to make a bar of chocolate; see how many connections you can make to your target language on this topic. Here is an extended sequence:

1. Give everyone in the class a piece of chocolate! There are several ways to do this:

   • Give everyone a chocolate, and while they smile and eat, have a brief discussion with questions like these:

   Do you like chocolate?

   What's your favorite brand of chocolate?

   What chocolate-flavored things do you eat? (ice cream, cake, etc.)

   Where is chocolate grown?

   Where is chocolate made?

   How is chocolate made?

   Follow this activity up with Step 2.

   • Have everyone take a handful of M&M's. For each one, they must write a sentence about chocolate, in the target language. Provide some helpful vocabulary on the board. Then go to Step 2.

   • Tell your students (the day before) that, as they enter the room, if they can tell you three reasons why they deserve a piece of chocolate, they may have one.

   Note: Whichever one of the above three you choose, the other two can be done later in the same unit; they are good activities any time!

2. To make the history connection, try an Internet web search: Give students questions to answer, and send them to one of the many good chocolate-oriented web sites. Figure 5.4 shows a sample worksheet, worth ten points.

   Some good chocolate web sites to use for this are:

   http://www.shoppingplace.com/chocolates/history.html and http://www.chocolate-alliance.com/history.php3 have good chocolate history sections.

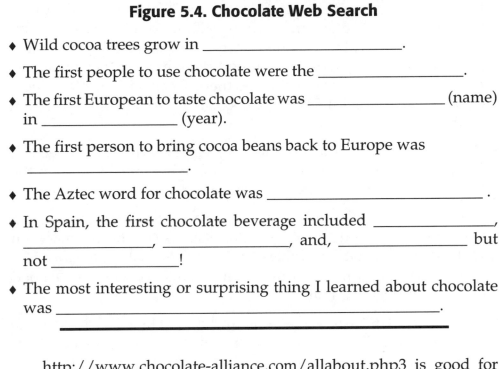

Figure 5.4. Chocolate Web Search

♦ Wild cocoa trees grow in _____.

♦ The first people to use chocolate were the _____.

♦ The first European to taste chocolate was _____ (name) in _____ (year).

♦ The first person to bring cocoa beans back to Europe was _____.

♦ The Aztec word for chocolate was _____ .

♦ In Spain, the first chocolate beverage included _____, _____, _____, and, _____ but not _____!

♦ The most interesting or surprising thing I learned about chocolate was _____.

http://www.chocolate-alliance.com/allabout.php3 is good for history, health facts, and so on.

http://home.talkcity.com/LetsDoLunchLn/death-by-chocolate/history.htm and http://www.5starchocolates.com/history/ have history and fun facts.

http://www.5starchocolates.com/history/#made, How Chocolate is Made, and http://www.virtualchocolate.com/bookhistory.cfm, list of "chocolate fiction," are both good for history, humor, and fun facts of chocolate.

Here follow some other Chocolate! activities:

♦ Spanish students can learn the following rhyme about pounding cacao beans into powder (such as for a mole sauce):

> Bate, bate chocolate, con arros y con tomate
> uno, dos, tres, CHO, uno, dos, tres, CO
> Uno, dos, tres, LA, uno, dos, tres, TE,
> Chocolate, chocolate, chocolate, chocolate!

♦ Show a video. Hershey's has a free educational movie, *The Chocolate Dream Machine*, in English, but you could make the worksheet in the TL. The gourmet cook Burt Wolfe also has a video on chocolate and its history.

♦ Here's how you can make the Science/ FACS connection: Go to the Cadbury's web site at http://www.cadbury.co.uk and read how chocolate is made. Have students list the steps, make an illustrated poster showing the steps, or do a short skit where one person mimes the steps while the partner narrates them. Click on Chocolate Encyclopedia, and then on Making Chocolate for excellent information on this process.

♦ To make the language arts connection, have students write poetry or short stories about chocolate. Some examples can be found on the Internet at http://wwwchocolatemuse.com.

♦ Take the Cadbury Chocolate Challenge to create a new kind of chocolate bar. Go to http://www.cadbury.co.uk/fr_enc.asp, click on History of Chocolate, and then on Chocolate Challenge. Have students create a wrapper and an ad campaign for it. Send in the good ones to Cadbury, for real.

♦ Have a chocolate tasting. Get as many different kinds of chocolate as possible, from TL country companies if you can. The web site at http://www.chocolate.com/chocolate_index.html has links to just about any country's chocolate. Here are some of the chocolate names you can find: in TL French, Suchard (France), Cote d'Or and Godiva (Belgium), or Lindt and Nestlé (Switzerland); in TL German, Ritter-Sport, Feodora, and Stollwerk; in TL Italian, Streglio; in TL Spanish, Ibarra (Mexico) and El Rey (Spain). Afterward, have students write about what they tasted, or do a survey and compile the results.

♦ Have a chocolate "festival": First, have students select chocolate recipes and translate them, either authentic ones from TL to English (examples in French, mousse, fondue; in Spanish, chocolate or mole sauce; in German, Black Forest cherry cake, and so on) or choose English ones to translate into the target language. Then, have students prepare the recipe of their choice and bring it to school. Play chocolate games (for example, "Hot and Cold" to find a chocolate, in the TL, of course). Elect a king and a queen after an interview during which they answer questions posed by the class. Deliver chocolate kisses to all the other faculty members on behalf of your language club.

♦ Homework projects:

  • Have students explain the origins of chocolate to a family member, or teach them the Chocolate chant, or prepare something authentic and chocolate, and bring back a brief description (or picture) of what was done, with a signature from the family member involved.

- Have them draw a Chocolate Timeline from when it was discovered to the present, with major developments listed.

- Have them create a chocolate game to play at the festival (suggested previously).

Another personalization activity has students discovering that many people's names are originally from another language, or perhaps discovering that there are different versions of the same name in every country (for example, Peter-Pierre-Pedro-Pietro-Pieter).

A Rose by Any Other Name ...: A Unit for Collecting Information on First and Last Names' Ethnicity

Have students find what their first and/or last name means, and what language it is from. (You can have them do their real first name, or, if it is one of the currently fashionable "creative" ones like N'Sheill, have them look up their classroom TL name, if you use those.)

For first names, begin with a dictionary. Many have a section on names in the back. If you have a book of the Name-Your-Baby type, this is good also. (There are usually inexpensive pocket-size versions of these at supermarket checkout lanes.)

Also try the web sites at http://www.engr.uvic.ca/~mcampbel/etym.html and http://gertrude.art.uiuc.edu/~ldzielak/neu/alfastart.html, or http://members.gnn.com/Hoefling/name.htm.

For last names, have students begin by asking their parents about what they know of the origin of the family name. (For example, a student named "Hemlock" found that the family had changed the Slavic "Hanulak" to something similar in English, so we looked up the Slavic name.) Many public libraries have interesting books on the origins of last names. Also, the first and last sites on the previous list allow students to research their last name. If theirs isn't there, they can send a request to the last one, which also contains historical information about the development of surnames.

To follow up, you may want to try a unit that will really create empathy for the non-American members of your community as well as highlight some aspects of their cultures and ours:

Immigration/Cultural Tolerance Unit

Have students take a map of the United States, and color in areas where people of their heritage settled. Under it, they should list why people emigrated from their respective countries, as well as the years that most arrived, and approximately how many. (They could also answer the question: "Did they find what they were expecting to find?") The data on ethnic groups' immigration patterns should be available in the library or online.

Have them also do a little research on their "heritage country." Have them list location, unique holidays or customs, traditional dress and food, currency used, and any interesting history or other information, in a brief essay in the TL.

As homework, and with parents' help, have them create a time line of their family's history that covers a hundred years. This may be done in any format, such as a storybook, a poster, a cartoon, and so on. Before assigning this, have the class brainstorm what a good time line should have: names, places (birth and death), jobs, any changes of location (from city to city or emigrations for example), weddings, any other family stories about important events. Then require the items they listed as desirable.

In class, take them to one of the many good Ellis Island sites on the Web such as http://www.ellisislandrecords.org/default.asp or the immigration links at http://davison.k12.mi.us/academic/immpage.htm, and help them find their family's arrival point.

Now, have them compare their lives to their grandfather's (or another relative's) lives, in at least nine different ways. This is a great exercise because it not only fosters family connections, but it requires them to use past tense verbs about Grandpa's experiences (written or oral, as you wish).

Have the students simulate the immigrant experience. Issue passports to your students, and partner up with another language class. For example, have your Spanish students interviewed in French by the students of the other class, who are trying to get their vital statistics (in French) to put down on a form. Then switch and have yours interview the French students, in Spanish, with a similar (but not identical) form. This will give them the experience that new arrivals with limited language proficiency have!

Then have your students take the test that resident aliens take to become American citizens, and see if they can pass it. Have them think what such a test might ask for citizenship in a target language country, and make a sample of such a test.

Finally, try to locate a portion of a movie about the immigrant experience, from a Charlie Chaplin segment in *Au revoir les enfants* to something like *Come See the Paradise* (Japanese immigrants at the beginning of World War II), to provide another opportunity to discuss cultural tolerance.

6

Standard 5: Communities

> ♦ Participate in Multilingual Communities at Home and Around the World
>
> • Standard 5.1: Students use the language both within and beyond the school setting
>
> • Standard 5.2: Students show evidence of becoming life-long learners by using the language for personal enjoyment and enrichment.

With this standard, which correlates with Standard 7 in Arizona, the goal is for students of the target language to participate in multilingual communities at home and around the world in a variety of contexts and in culturally appropriate ways. A teacher should therefore ask the following questions:

♦ What opportunities do students have to use the language outside the classroom?

♦ What community resources can be brought into the classroom to enrich the language and cultural experiences for students?

♦ How much technology can be used to facilitate communication of students beyond the classroom wall?

Two Words to Remember

The most important word to remember, in this standard or for any standard, is the word "life." We should wish most of all to give our students something to take away from our classroom that will stay with them for their entire lives, that will help them in their chosen career, that will enrich their lives in many ways. It is this desire that Standard 5 addresses.

But because it is such a long-range goal we are setting, and one that is both affective and subjective, I'd suggest that success in this goal will be very close to impossible to evaluate ... and so perhaps we should not even try. We should just assess competence on the short-term parts (Did students understand the point being made in the discussion? Do they comprehend the need to help the community they live in?), and not worry about the long term effects. Those are the kinds of things we will be able to assess only during occasional encounters with former students at sporting events, in a store, or at the beach, when they reminisce about things remembered from class that they've used or done since. And so I would suggest that the second word to remember when addressing this standard is the word "inspire."

Ways in Which You are Probably Already Implementing This Standard

- Penpals
- Field trips to museums, plays or restaurants
- Movies in target language
- Web searches
- Student/school exchange program
- Making traditional foods
- Peer tutoring
- Guest speakers (especially native TL speakers)
- Songs
- Career opportunities unit
- Trips abroad
- Units on health/welfare and ecology

Standard 5.1

Students use the language both within and beyond the school setting.

Language as a tool for communication is the basic idea here, and the main focus of a teacher implementing Standard 5.1 would be to show students as many different ways the language will be useful *outside the classroom*, both within and beyond the school walls, in the community and abroad. Doing so should make the advantages of speaking a second language obvious, and desirable.

Within the School Walls

The most obvious way to bring the foreign language out is through presentations (see Standard 1.3 for many implementations). With many lessons, students have a culminating activity that results in a product, which they take out into the rest of the school or into the community, such as putting on a play or having a poetry slam.

Poetry Slams

A poetry slam is an oral poetry competition. In a slam, the idea is to not just read the poem, but to perform it and to give the audience the chance to openly react to, and interact with, the poet on stage. In my version, each poet performs an original spoken word piece for no more than three minutes. (Points are deducted for running overtime.) Judges, chosen randomly from the audience, score the poets from 1 to 10 and at the end, a winner is chosen and awarded a prize. Rules include no props, no music, and no costumes.

Judging is not based on poetic skill as much as the communicative and/or entertainment value that the poem offers. A slam has more of a party atmosphere with the audience free to jump up and make comments, both positive or negative. (But there is a no-put-down-of-the-speaker rule, however; comments must deal only with a poem's message or content.)

Slams are becoming extremely popular on college campuses and in larger cities; I've even seen a few on television. There are even traveling teams, as well as a U.S. National Slam (and a Canadian one, too, I believe).

School Celebrations

For National Foreign Language week, my students label everything in the building in our target language (French) and go on the closed circuit daily school newscasts with a song, a dance, a music video, a poem, or a bit of trivia. We also do our annual Warm Fuzzies:

Warm Fuzzies

Get a list of every adult worker in your building/district (don't forget the school board, too) and have your students send them a thank you for all they do. If the person can read the TL, they'll thank the student(s) and if not, they'll make contact to see what it says! Everyone likes compliments.

For National French Week in November, we do even more. First, we have a Greetings Day. I pick one Mystery Adult on our staff, and have a prize for the first student to greet that person in French. We also have the Teach a Friend program. I give each student a coupon with his/her name on it. If he or she teaches a friend to say "Hello, how are you?" in French to me, and gives me his or her coupon, I not only give the friend a lollipop, but the student-teacher gets an extra credit point. We prepare and sell crepes during lunch hour on another day, and have an after-school movie-and-popcorn day. We also have a week-long Scavenger Hunt.

Scavenger Hunt

Language: This is written for French, but by changing the language, it is applicable to any language and any level.

On or before Friday, bring in as many of the following items as possible:

1. A French word or phrase seen on TV, with date, time, channel, and program watched.

2. A French word or phrase heard in a song in English, taped, or bring in the CD.

3. A printout of an Internet page on a French topic or in French (one page only!)

4. A French coin (or a Euro) or a French postage stamp.

5. A postcard of a French-speaking region of the world.

6. The name of a local business that does business with a French-speaking country.

7. The name and telephone number of a person in the community not associated with the school system, who speaks French.

8. A French food served at a local restaurant (name of food and where served).

9. A painting you saw that was painted by a French artist, and where you saw it (ones in school buildings don't count!), or draw a copy of one from an art book.

10. A piece of clothing with a label (inside or outside) written in French.

11. A box or bag with instructions written in French (Note: not a list of ingredients).

12. A crossword puzzle that asks for a French word as one of the entries.

13. A newspaper article about an event in France or a French-speaking country.

14. A recipe for some authentic French food.

15. An item that says "Made in France."

16. Attend a cultural event in French, or about France, and bring back proof of attendance: ticket stub or program. Events might be a museum show, movie, play, concert, religious service, dance, or see me to find out if another event might qualify.

The above list would be excellent to use for extra credit for a class. Choose one per week, and give anyone who locates that item during that week an extra credit point, a coupon, a piece of candy, or whatever reward you usually use for above-and-beyond-the-call-of-duty efforts.

Still within school walls, technically, would be a visit to another school. Our high-school students recently sang Christmas carols and talked about holiday customs at the nearby middle school, taking them an authentic-recipe "bûche de Noël" to eat as well. In the spring, my advanced class will write and illustrate a children's book (they choose from traditional, pop-up, lift-the-flap, and several other styles) in French, and go to the nearby elementary school to read it to a group of students. Some of our Spanish students are enlisted to help elementary Hispanic children with their studies after school.

Exchange Student Awareness Unit

Start by having students interview the exchange and Hispanic students in the school, finding out where they are from and why they came to America. Have students give a summary of the information they found out in either written or oral form to the class. Mark on a map where each is from. (Many people believe the Hispanics are all Mexican, and the students may be in for a surprise.)

Invite the exchange students that speak the target language to speak to your class. Have students prepare and submit questions they'd like to ask the day before the speaker arrives, to avoid any embarrassments. Have students write a thank-you note to the speaker(s), stating their feelings about what the student(s) said.

Spanish classes have a special opportunity. *Contacto Magazine* publishes an annual special edition about Hispanics in the United States. The articles, all in Spanish, may be found at http://www.contactomagazine.com/.

Try some cultural awareness activities that may surprise your students:

- Check local stores for the number of white vs. ethnic dolls available.
- Check the local and school libraries for books written in languages other than English.
- Check the number of school employees who are nonwhite (and compare with the percentage of students).
- Watch the local news and see how many broadcasters are nonwhite, and how many news stories deal with minorities.
- Watch network television and check out the number of minority actors as compared with whites.

Have your students write a short essay and make a poster to go with it. Post in the school halls.

Here's an activity that I haven't tried yet for myself but have seen colleagues try, and that our school has discussed doing soon on a school-wide basis:

Model United Nations

Level: Upper Intermediate or Advanced, if in target language

May be done within a class, or within the school district, or as an interdisciplinary unit with either a speech class or social studies.

The basic idea is to pick an international issue such as pollution, peace, immigration, economic stability, or human rights, and to conduct a mock debate as follows (or with variations to fit your situation):

1. Divide students into groups, with each group representing a different country. Your students would, of course, represent different countries that speak the target language.

2. Students then work individually or in groups to collect information on their country, especially regarding its current situation, its background (causes), and the country's current needs and wants regarding the debate topic. If given enough time, students should be able to communicate directly with the embassy of this country for detailed information.

3. Students then write speeches (in the target language would be best; they may supply an "interpreter" if addressing groups from nontarget language countries) expressing their country's situation and what they would like to see done about it.

4. As students present these speeches to the General Assembly of nations, all students fill in a graphic organizer with the pertinent facts contained in each speech.

5. All introductory speeches concluded, students refer to the information on their grid to agree or disagree with the proposals of each nation. The group must try to agree on their priorities of which issues to address first.

6. The groups adjourn briefly to come up with possible solutions for the most serious problems (the highest priorities) and return to propose these to the general group in a question-and-answer format. Individual countries may sign agreements to cooperate on some of these solutions.

7. As a good follow-up activity, have students write an essay about an important issue and the solution they would like to see for that problem.

Assessing this activity could be done on several levels, with the rubrics set up ahead of time and either presented to the students, or developed by the students. Some factors to assess include the following:

♦ Quality of input (data vs. opinion)

♦ Quality of persuasiveness (good speaking skills, clear proposals)

♦ Use of target language exclusively

♦ Reviewing the grids filled out to assess listening comprehension

Within the Community

Because students will not always remain within school walls, it is important to help them learn opportunities the community offers to use the target language.

Make a Brochure

Have students make a brochure or pamphlet for distribution throughout the community to visitors from TL countries or for new arrivals to the community. Here are some ideas:

♦ Create publicity for your school. Locate authentic ads for schools in a TL country (authentic material) and have students prepare similar ones. This can be done by beginning classes, if you use a bullet format that is a list of noun-plus-adjective phrases: many sports, good teachers, and so on. Put them up in the halls; most of them will have a lot of cognates, so other students can see how their school is special, in the target language. (And some students may even be encouraged to try your class!) Offer the ads to the school board or chamber of commerce, or post them in areas where immigrants could see them (local literacy council, Well Child clinic, and so on). These can take the form of posters as well, or can be added, with a special button (a flag of a TL country) to your school's web site.

♦ Provide information about your community. My students examine brochures about our area: the county, the city, medical institutions, or individual businesses (for example, stores like Wal-Mart, bed-and-breakfast establishments, flea markets, amusement parks). They should choose something that a newcomer to the community would want to know about and which might be helpful to them. After researching the materials available in English as well as the history of the business (including an interview with the owner), they prepare their own (in French), as part of a career unit (career as a translator), and offer the resulting document to the subject of their study. Another interesting twist on this would be to research the history of a particular building, and write a brief history of it, presenting a clean copy to the owners of the building (city, local college campus, historic home, and so on), who are generally happy (or at least, intrigued) to have a document about their building.

◆ Prepare something for a nearby (international) corporation. Choose one of their products, and have students describe the product, and develop a sales campaign. Have the company judge the results. Or, offer to translate materials the company already has in English, as a community service.

You will find a long list of community service projects in the second portion of this standard because, in teaching students about these and having them experience the fulfillment of community service, I aspire to create a lifelong commitment to and enjoyment of such activities. So, I have chosen to place these under Standard 5.2.

Abroad

We all know about the value of pen pals, but here are a few more words on the subject, and perhaps a few applications you haven't thought of yet.

Friendships through the Written Word

The best motivator for using the TL for communication is, hands down, a pen pal or a keypal. I love to see students gain a new friend for life in this way, and they often share items of interest written by their correspondent. Send letters, e-mail, pictures, or even videos (though those will need to be transcoded for viewing). There are many Internet or snail-mail addresses that provide correspondents for interested students, but here are a few I've tried that worked well:

◆ Go to http://www.epals.com to match your entire class up with another. Contact the teacher and set up a schedule for corresponding, topics for each month, and so on. There is no cost for this. You can also set up a completely private chat room to meet with the other class, live (despite different time zones), and have a live chat. My students absolutely love doing this! Because we are paired with an English class in France, we switch languages every ten minutes. To give the conversations a start (and provide some direction), I give my students a list of questions to find answers for each time (for example, surveys on current events, fads, favorite vacation sites, birthday presents, or whatever topic we're working on at the time).

- For Spanish, try the Nueva Alejandria site from Argentina at http://www.nalejandria.com/index.htm. Click on Clases Gemelas to be paired up with mostly South American schools.

- For slightly more anonymous but highly motivating forms of communication, find a message board site such as my favorite, the Viv@ (Virtual Interactive Village in the Ardèche) in which students from all over the world write collaborative stories, share opinions on music, movies, books, and more. Post a statement or answer one, and then check back every week or so to see if someone has answered your posting. Viv@'s address is http://www.ardecol.ac-grenoble.fr/viva/index.htm. So far, postings have been in English, French, Portuguese, Italian, and, I think, a little bit of Romanian. The rule is that postings must be answered in the language of the original posting, so you could easily add your target language to this site.

Cards and E-Cards

Have students send a family member, an exchange student, a keypal or a friend an e-card in the target language (have them send you a copy). Here are some good e-card addresses for foreign languages.

- French
  - http://cartespourenfants.com
  - http://perso.infonie.fr/accl/postcard.htm
  - http://www.dromadaire.com/fr/
  - http://cartes.sympatico.ca/
- German: http://german.about.com/library/blpostkarte.htm
- Italian: http://www.isol.it/postcard/
- Japanese: http://perso.libertysurf.fr/o11jb/cards/cartes.htm
- Portuguese http://cardbrasil.com/
- Spanish
  - http://www.correomagico.com
  - http://www.ciberpostales.com/
  - http://tarjetasvirtuales.com/galerias.htm
  - http://egreetings.com
  - http://www.latincards.com

As for regular handmade cards, here are some ideas that go beyond the "Give it to Mom" one:

♦ Find a nursing home, a homeless shelter, Meals on Wheels for shut-ins, or another similar center of concern and donate yours for distribution to brighten someone's day. Sometimes hospitals will take them for patients' trays, too. I have a nursing home address in Quebec that we send Valentines to every year, and my students take extra care on theirs because they know it is going to a native speaker who will really appreciate it. (I got the address from a local church; they are a good resource for this.)

♦ Punch a hole in the corner of your cards, string them with ribbon or yarn, and use them (plus Ojos de Dio or another traditional ornament) to decorate a tree for a nursing home, hospital, or armed services base in the area. Later, visit and sing carols, or send a tape of your students singing in the target language.

♦ Send your cards to "pals" in an elementary-school class you visit from time to time.

♦ Draw "secret pals" with another language class and send notes and cards.

♦ Have a contest for the best designs, print them out, attach a lollipop, and sell in the school bookstore for 25 cents (or take orders and deliver them all on a given day such as February 14th, with messages the purchasers have written inside). This is a good fundraiser for some of the community service projects you'll find later in this chapter.

♦ If possible, get college addresses for last year's seniors; have your advanced group send them a card or even begin a correspondence.

Other Ideas

Here are more ideas to help students realize how many target language resources are out there, easy to find:

♦ Have first-year students make a scrapbook in which they collect and label at least ten examples of target language or culture: labels, instructions, pamphlets, headlines, and so on. (See the Scavenger Hunt idea earlier in the chapter for more suggestions.)

♦ Take a close look at groups that speak the target language in this country. For German teachers, why not look at the Amish? See material about them on the Internet at http://www.goethe.de/uk/chi/netz/amish.htm. French teachers can look at Cajun culture, and so on.

Standard 5.2

Students show evidence of becoming life-long learners by using the language for personal enjoyment and enrichment.

Most Americans spend their leisure time reading, listening to music, watching television or movies, or interacting with each other. Standard 5.2 asks us to prepare students to include the target language in these activities for their entire lives by accessing various entertainment and information sources available only to people who know the target language. The focus is on the word "enjoyment," so the first step is to find out what students' interests are; then, we teach them what target resources are out there that enhance or appeal to those interests.

Another thing we can do is to open them to new interests and ideas; this is, for me, the enjoyable part of this standard. Expose your students to new ideas, and widen their perspective on the world.

Here is a short list of the ways most often used to address this standard, all of them undoubtedly obvious (but good) applications. Most of these are field trips:

Travel abroad	Visit a museum
Attend a movie	Visit a restaurant
Attend a sporting event	Cook/try new foods
Attend a play or dance performance	Read periodicals in the target language

My favorite method of applying this standard is to expose students to authentic music, as well as children's rhymes, finger plays (songs or rhymes built around physical motions), and poems. Not only will they like these and beg to do them again and again, but these commonplace things learned in the target language (and they are easy to learn) can echo in their minds for years. Hearing a bit of a song in the soundtrack of a movie will bring back memories of the target language, or perhaps create a common bond with a native speaker later in life. All the above methods will develop language skills as well as cultural insights.

Use the cultural resources of your community (theaters, museums, libraries, historic sites, and performing arts groups) to create opportunities for your students to expand their appreciation of the target language and the target culture. Here are some more suggestions.

Coffee Talk

One of my favorite things in college was to go practice my conversational skills with other speakers of the language.

If your area doesn't already have a foreign language coffee hour, check with local coffeehouses (or bookstores) about setting up one evening once or twice a month for people to have a Target Language Conversational night. They are usually quite cooperative about scheduling these, especially if you can get the local paper to publicize these events.

Either require students to attend once a month, or give extra credit for attendance. Try to get performers whenever possible: play TL music, organize a poetry reading or a poetry slam (after writing poems in class), get students to sing or do a reading from a play … or just come have coffee and chat in the TL in a relaxed, comfortable setting. You may even get other community members who show up for these, often native speakers or people who lived abroad.

Another option to explore would be to start a reading group. Choose a book in the target language that could also be available in translation, and have discussions.

The Games People Play

Teach games that students can continue to play all their lives.

♦ Sports: Before it got popular, I would teach them soccer. Now, I coach the school's traveling pétanque team; we have uniforms, belong to the national organization (http://www.petanque-usa.org) and host one or two meets per season with area schools.

♦ Card games: Introduce your card players to authentic games. "Tarot" is an extremely popular French game. Parker Brothers' Mille Bornes game is another they like to play.

♦ Board games: Play Twister, Scrabble, Pictionary, Trivial Pursuit, the Ungame, or others in the target language.

♦ Let's not forget hobbies! Have a show-and-tell day once a month when selected students bring in and demonstrate a hobby or interest of theirs, in the target language.

Community Service

Help your students experience the fulfillment that comes from helping another person, by giving them the opportunity to become involved with community service projects on a local, national or international level. Even better, choose these projects so they enable students to use their target language skills for reading, writing, or speaking, thereby crossing cultural frontiers as well.

One word of advice: check with your department chair and/or principal to make sure this project is okay and that they are aware that you are doing this. Some of the more "activist" ideas might provoke opposition from someone; in those cases, of course, you don't need to make participation mandatory.

- ♦ Local service projects

  - Help persons newly arrived in your community (from a TL country or region) by volunteering as a guide to the community; help them register children for school, locate doctors, churches and other local landmarks.

  - Serve as informal interpreters for people needing to make telephone calls for information about needed services (getting a driving license, a green card, and so on).

  - Provide transportation to and serve as informal interpreters for families to medical, dental, and social service appointments.

  - Provide childcare at specified times (for example, while parents take English classes).

  - Organize a once-a-week class for English practice, and invite people who would like help.

  - Younger children could color paper bags with English lessons, holiday sayings, and so on, for use by groups distributing food, toiletries, and other items to the needy or to elderly shut-ins, or for delivery of someone's meal.

  - Tutor new students from other countries who need help with school subjects in their native language while they learn English here.

  - Call the Coalition for Literacy 1-800-228-8813 to get in touch with your local literacy coalition, and teach someone to read.

  - Co-host a cultural festival (perhaps for a holiday) in conjunction with TL speakers in the community.

  - Translate brochures related to health care and social services and distribute them to TL speakers.

  - Adopt a needy family and visit them once a month, taking birthday gifts, groceries, or other needed items.

  - Organize and deliver donations of groceries, clothing (for example, warm winter coats and boots), toys, and furniture so that they are easily accessible.

- Provide a free meal for a special holiday.
- Work in a soup kitchen.

Students may not, at first, be entirely enthusiastic about doing community service. You must decide to either require it, or to give extra credit for it. I have tried both ways. When I required participation, I also required a one-page self-reflective paper about the experience: what was done, by whom, with whom, and when, and how they felt about the experience, including suggestions to improve it. Using the extra credit method did not get as many volunteers on specific days (for example, for delivery projects) but the volunteers were much more committed and more likely to continue the activity even when extra credit wasn't involved (during the summer months).

- ◆ National level service

  - Help a nationally organized club. Kiwanis and Rotary frequently have World Community or International projects organized. Contact a local chapter for ideas and needs.

  - Participate in Make a Difference Day, held yearly toward the end of October. Information on this day in Spanish is available on the Web at http://www.usaweekend.com/diffday/diffday_spanish.html.

- ◆ International service projects

Many international aid organizations exist to address different sorts of needs. Here are some we have worked with, all nonprofit organizations:

- Help out other schools in needy areas.

  - ◆ Donate old books in English and ship them abroad for students learning English. Pick a country and contact their teachers' association for the address of a needy school.

  - ◆ Try the Clean Your Desk Campaign. (We change it to Clean Your Locker.) Put out collection boxes during locker cleaning time at your school, for new and used school supplies. Half a bottle of glue or a used eraser can be donated to children who need them, which is what this organization does. Contact: Quixote Center/Quest for Peace, Clean Your Desk Campaign, PO Box 5206, Hyattsville, MD 20782, Telephone 301-669-0042. They will send you intermediate-level lesson plans and posters for teaching about Nicaragua and the project in your classrooms. They also tell you how to pack the supplies and what they need along with posters and address labels.

- Help organizations that combat poverty and hunger.
  - ◆ We all know about UNICEF, the United Nations Children's Emergency Fund. And yes, trick-or-treating for UNICEF is still being done. Contact them at http://www.unicef.org/. It is possible to read this site in French and Spanish, too.
  - ◆ Oxfam received the Nobel Prize for Peace for its efforts to "find solutions to poverty, hunger and social injustice" (from a recent mailing). Not only does this group provide food during a famine, but they send out specialists to dig wells and irrigate, teach hygiene or better crop planting methods, or train locals in new crafts that will generate income—in other words, not just fill a need, but help to prepare for a better future. Contact them at http://www.oxfamamerica.org. This site has "field trips" (articles with pictures) to many areas on the globe where they are working, and it is possible to get information in French, Spanish, and a few other languages.
  - ◆ NetAid supplies clean, safe water and other forms of aid. See http://www.netaid.org. In the "Kids Can Help" section it says, "Learn to draw, create, speak your mind, connect, make a difference" and right now on this site there is an article titled "Seventh Graders Make a Difference" about a class in Maine's efforts to help in Burkina Faso (French-speaking area of Africa).
  - ◆ The Heifer Project International provides animals or tree seedlings to "help families around the world become self-reliant" and training to insure that the plants and animals stay healthy and productive. You can also send personal notes of encouragement along with your gift(s). Call 1-800-422-0755 or go online at http://www.heifer.org.
  - ◆ Help the environment, have fun, and win a party. Every year Chiquita Bananas has the Eco-kid Challenge, with the winners getting a contribution to Allies in the Rainforest, a locally based Latin American environmental group that works with the Rainforest Alliance, the world's leading advocate for rainforest preservation. The online address is http://www.chiquitakids.com/learnit/ecokid_challenge.asp.
- Help during times of need: hurricane relief, earthquakes, war.
  - ◆ Doctors without Borders also received the Nobel Peace Prize for its efforts to provide medical care for the needy in war-torn areas of the globe, most recently in Bosnia and Afghanistan. Imagine how following their actions would enliven a study of current

events. This group originated in France as MSF (Médecins sans Frontières). The American office is online at http://www. dwb.org. Under "Exhibits" are teacher's resources, lesson plans on famine relief, refugee issues, and the Nobel Prize. Each of these would easily connect to other subject areas.

♦ Mission Honduras: This group works in an area regularly devastated by natural disasters. Contact information: Mission Honduras, 433 Aullwood Road, Salina, KS 67401, Telephone 785-825-1703.

- Join groups to preserve human rights around the globe.

  ♦ As a longtime member of AI (Amnesty International), I formed a school chapter of this nonpolitical group that also received the Nobel Peace Prize. Amnesty International works to uphold basic human rights, and so has many different activities to choose from. We choose to participate in the Urgent Action movement, so once a month we receive information about someone or a group whose human rights are being violated, and we write letters on their behalf to government officials in that country. This is a good learning experience as we look at where the country is on the globe, learn its rulers' names, and hear about conflicts that often don't receive coverage on American television. We can often write letters in the target language (for example, in French to various African countries, in Spanish to South American ones). And imagine our sense of fulfillment when we learn one of "our" cases has been able to receive visitors, medical care, legal assistance, or even been released. Students can attend regional student conferences, and most college campuses have active AI chapters. Contact Amnesty International at http://www.amnesty-usa.org. They also offer Children's Action, which features cases where children are threatened. AI can also get you materials to use in various target languages.

- Join groups dealing with ecological issues.

  ♦ The most obvious group for FL classes might be Greenpeace, though sometimes their political stance is rather aggressive. I say "obvious" because they have their own web sites in many languages (www.greenpeace.fr, French; www.greenpeace.it, Italian; www.greenpeace.es, Spanish; www.greenpeace.de, German) and sites for many other countries, including Greece, Israel, Japan and China. More information on those may be found at http://www.greenpeace.org/.

♦ The Rainforest Alliance is an international nonprofit organization dedicated to the conservation of tropical forests for the benefit of the global community. The web site is at http://www.rainforest-alliance.org.

Net-Escape

The Internet is here to stay, and people of all ages enjoy what it has to offer. In addition to educational sites, why not introduce your students to the more recreational aspects available in the target language?

Perhaps you'd like to start with the many "Why Take (Target Language)?" sites. When your students say, "How will this language ever be useful to me?" they'll find an answer here at http://eleaston.com/why.html#ws, which lists hundreds of sites, or to individual sites.

I have my favorite reasons for French on my web site at http://www.msdsteuben.k12.in.us/dblaz/newpage2.htm but there's a take-french web site from GlobeGate at http://fmc.utm.edu/~rpeckham/profren.html.

For Spanish, try http://www.amerispan.com.

For German, http://www.muc.edu/~himmelm/why/main.html or "Auf Deutsch!" at http://www.goethe.de/i/deiazeh.htm.

Italian is at http://www.cas.usf.edu/languages/whystudy/whyital.htm.

Japanese, at http://www.bgsu.edu/departments/greal/Japan-why.html.

Portuguese, at http://www.ukans.edu/~spanport/reasons.html.

Russian is at http://www.russnet.org/why/index.html.

Humor sites such as http://www.solochistes.com/estupideces.htm or http://www.bepop.com.ar/humor/ (Spanish), http://www.blagues.net (French), and so on offer all sorts of jokes. (Be careful for content; these sites aren't bad, but there are always a few.) There are also silly sites, like the MENJ (Front for the Liberation of Garden Gnomes) site in French, http://www.menj.com that even offers t-shirts (some of my students have them!), or "Adopt an Escargot" (http://www.adoptanescargot.com/). Those you'll have to look for on your own.

Games and recreational sites: For games, try sites like http://juegos.hispavista.com/ or http://fr.games.yahoo.com/. Spanish teachers would like the site http://www.disneylatino.com, which has lots of games to explore there. (Try Pooh y Yo, for example.) There are also full color maps to the Disney parks with descriptions of the attractions in Spanish. You could do an interesting "fantasy visit" unit with this, and write imaginary postcards afterward. Also worth a try is "Mexico para Niños" at http://www.elbalero.gob.mx/ index_esp.html.

Keypals and chat areas: Again, I recommend getting the administration's okay on this, but http://www.epals.com is a safe (monitored) way to get correspondents for your students and link up with classes all over the world. The Viv@ site for posting messages and creative writing opportunities at http://www.ardecol.ac-grenoble.fr/viva/index.htm.

Current events/Research engines: Take a server like Yahoo and try typing the country code at the end: www.yahoo.fr (France), www.yahoo.it (Italy), www.yahoo.es (Spain), www.yahoo.de (Germany), and so on. These offer games, current events, and many other things as well as the research engine.

Careers for the Future

Using the target language during employment is perhaps the best way for students to realize its value, and appreciate learning it. Remind your students to put "Speak (TL)" on all job applications to give them an edge.

Here are some ways (some common, and some less so) to involve students in learning about, and perhaps finding, a career using the TL:

♦ Have students send out letters to every business and social service agency in the community as a survey to see which use the TL on the job, do business in the TL, are owned by a TL company, and so on.

♦ Have students interview members of the community (on video, if possible) who use the TL for personal (perhaps travel, sports, or crafts) or professional reasons. Then have them do oral, visual (video), or written reports about the interview. If possible, have them job shadow the person while they are working.

♦ Invite selected people who use the TL (perhaps having students select the more interesting-sounding ones from the activity described in the previous bulleted section) to speak to the class in the TL about what they do. Have the class prepare questions to ask in the TL, but have them submit those to you a day ahead, so there are no embarrassments.

♦ Have students, individually or in small groups, write thank you notes to the speakers who visit the classroom, mentioning their reactions to the speech as well as their personal future plans.

♦ Have students, individually or in small groups, do the worksheet depicted in Figure 6.1. I do this sometimes like Scattergories, in which the writing portion is timed and then students receive points for any application they thought of which was not thought of by any other groups.

Figure 6.1. Careers Worksheet

Brainstorm possible uses for French in the following career areas. Write as many as you can think of:

1. Retail (stores and businesses)
2. Finance (banking, etc.)
3. Transportation
4. Medicine
5. Law (including police)
6. Tourism
7. Politics
7. Journalism/writing
8. Sports
9. Art
10. Food
11. Service industry

♦ Have students look at help-wanted ads in newspapers, such as *France-Amérique* or *La Raza*, which are aimed at a TL speaking populations, and see if there are any interesting-sounding jobs.

♦ Have students go online to job sites, type in the target language as the keyword for a search, and see the hundreds of jobs that pop up. Have them list their favorite jobs, salaries, and reasons why they like these. Here are some good job search sites to use: http://monster.com, http://headhunter.net, and http://hotjobs.com.

♦ Have students select a profession, and make a poster, with the name of the profession (in the TL) and an illustration (original, clip art, or cut-and-pasted from a magazine) prominently featured, followed by a list of ten job duties for that profession. The grammar used could be set up to use a particular language structure. (I'll give Spanish, with French in parentheses.) First year could say "*Voy a ____*" (*aller* plus infinitive). Second-year students might write "*Si soy ____, trabajare con____*" (if...then structure) and more advanced could use "*Si fuera ____, trabajaria ____*" (future and conditional).

♦ Here are a couple alternatives to the above assignment. Instead of a poster, have students tape themselves saying their list, and give the class a list of students' names, having them list each profession chosen and one duty from the list they hear (a good listening and writing activity). If you have voice mail, have your students call you over the weekend, and tell you what they'd like to be and why (but not identify themselves), and play back the messages, having the class guess who that was who was speaking.

♦ Do a vocabulary-building unit such as this one that I wrote one summer. Pick any retail business; I chose JoAnn's Fabrics and Crafts because that is my weekend job.

Careers in Retail

Goals: Students will practice their job application skills in French. Students will learn some jobs not covered in their text, but common in retail stores.

Procedure: All activities will be done in French.

1. Students will brainstorm types of jobs to be found at JoAnn's Fabrics and Crafts with the teacher, resulting in the following list: stocker, cashier, cutter, department specialist, team member, manager, assistant manager.

2. For each job, list duties. For example, a cashier should smile, push buttons, scan items, greet customers, accept payment, give change, do refunds, put things in bags, and so on.

3. Students will then choose the position they feel most qualified for, and list the skills they have that will help them at that job.

4. The class will then watch a video of a job interview in French, taking notes on how the student behaved, what sorts of information they were required to give, and what sorts of questions were asked by the interviewer.

5. Have students read a letter of application for a job, and call their attention to culturally appropriate aspects of it, such as the formal salutation and closing.

6. In a discussion, the class will review that students need to be able to discuss the following: previous experience (if any), interests or skills they have related to this job, hours and days they will be available to work and when they can start, salary desired, and cultural differences in greetings, saying please and thank you, and so on.

7. Students will complete a job application, in French, listing the position they will interview for.

8. Students will have either an oral or a written interview with the teacher for a final grade.

When I assign Step 8, I also give them a copy of the rubric to be used (Figure 6.2, p. 136). I generally use a checklist as it is simplest to fill out as I listen, and as it is usually something similar to what an employer/interview might use.

A Final Encouragement

This standard should not be neglected; life-long learning, personal enrichment, and enjoyment using the target language are the skills, learned in your classroom, that will make students desire and appreciate all the other things about the language, for the rest of their lives.

Figure 6.2. Career Project Rubrics

Rubric for Oral Interview: 10 pts.

_____ Culturally appropriate greeting

_____ Began conversation

_____ Stated position desired

_____ Stated qualifications/skills

_____ Stated experience

_____ Stated availability

_____ Thanked employer for interview

_____ Asked a question

_____ Used correct grammar

_____ Used correct pronunciation

Rubric for Written Application: 10 pts.

_____ Used correct, formal salutation

_____ Wrote/typed neatly (no crossouts, good margins, etc.)

_____ Stated position/salary desired

_____ Stated previous experience

_____ Stated skills and qualifications for the job

_____ Stated dates and times available to work

_____ Gave information for contacting him/her

_____ Used culturally appropriate ending to letter

_____ Used correct grammar

_____ Used correct spelling

7

Textbook Evaluation

Evaluating a textbook based upon the five Cs is an important aspect of implementing these standards in your classroom. This chapter presents formatted questions that can be used to evaluating a text. They are a synthesis of input from colleagues, my own personal views on what I look for in a text, an examination of various materials put out by textbook publishers touting the strengths of their own particular texts, and textbook evaluation forms given to me by curriculum directors at the local and state level here in Angola, IN.

Along with the evaluation of the text, you will note that in certain sections you are also asked to evaluate the ancillaries. Workbooks, overheads, video and audio tapes, teacher materials, CD-ROMs, publishers' web site activities, and tests form an integral part of the learning experience, too, and should not be overlooked. I think that tests especially should be carefully examined. What good is a test if it does not test the material in the text in the same manner it was practiced?

In every section, the rating scale shown in Figure 7.1 should apply.

Figure 7.1. Book Questions Rating Scale

4	3	2	1
Very much	Adequate	Less than I'd like	Almost none

I strongly recommend the use of a four-point rating scale because it is impossible to give a rating exactly in the middle of the scale. A decision must be made as to whether a text series falls on the positive or negative side of the spectrum.

Standard 1: Communication

Communication should be covered through oral, written, listening, and presentational activities. Examine the text and workbook first for activities that involve the *oral production of the target language* (interpersonal mode) and *present it to others* (presentational mode). See Figure 7.2

Figure 7.2. Oral Production and Presentation Questions

Does this text allow/encourage students to	Text X	Text Y	Text Z
☐ Interact with each other verbally, in pairs or in groups?			
☐ Provide details of their own lives?			
☐ Talk about topics that are age-appropriate?			
☐ Vary the form and structure (grammar)?			
☐ Simulate a real-world context or task?			
☐ Elaborate their response?			
TOTAL			

Now, examine several sections in which the student is asked to *read a selection* and react to it, or *listen to a conversation* and respond (interpretive mode). See Figure 7.3.

Figure 7.3. Interpretive Mode Questions

Do the selected activities	Text X	Text Y	Text Z
☐ Present information (vocabulary, structures) in functional, thematic units?			
☐ Allow students to demonstrate their ability to apply different learning strategies to successfully comprehend the selection?			
☐ Provide guidance and/or hints to aid comprehension?			
☐ Use language that is authentic, accurate, and current?			
☐ Appeal to students' interests?			
TOTAL			

Finally, locate several activities that require a *written response* from students (presentational mode again). See Figure 7.4.

Figure 7.4. Written Presentation Questions

Do the activities permit the student to	Text X	Text Y	Text Z
☐ Demonstrate mastery of the vocabulary and structures in this unit?			
☐ Write a response that should differ from student to student based upon the students' life styles and interests?			
☐ Know how their work will be evaluated (rubrics, clear instructions) and are expectations reasonable?			
TOTAL			

Standard 2: Cultures

Remember the three Ps of Culture: Practices, Products, and Perspectives. First, find and examine several visuals: overheads, book illustrations, or videos. See Figure 7.5.

Figure 7.5. Culture Questions for Visual Materials

Are the visuals:	Text X	Text Y	Text Z
☐ Attractive and inviting?			
☐ Current?			
☐ Authentic?			
☐ Age-appropriate to stimulate interest?			
☐ Depictions of both "big-C" and "little-c" culture?			
☐ Depictions of a variety of peoples and cultures that speak the target language?			
☐ Well integrated with the theme or text of the section?			
TOTAL			

Then, look at the designated Culture sections in the text, both small and large, and in the workbook (generally found in the readings section). See Figure 7.6.

Figure 7.6. Questions about Content of Culture Sections

Do these selections	Text X	Text Y	Text Z
☐ Depict culture that is significant?			
☐ Depict culture that is current?			
☐ Depict culture in an accurate manner?			
☐ Depict culture that is age-appropriate to stimulate interest?			
☐ Depict a variety of peoples and cultures that speak the target language?			
☐ Include practices such as games, songs, celebrations, stories, sports, and entertainment representative of target language culture(s)?			
☐ Identify products: toys, dress, foods, art, songs, literature?			
☐ Include information on how students can discuss or produce these products themselves?			
☐ Encourage discussion of the perspectives of the target language culture reflected in these practices and products, without encouraging stereotypes?			
☐ Include sources written for native speakers?			
TOTALS			

Standard 3: Connections

Look through the text and ancillaries to locate activities that encourage students to connect their foreign language skills and knowledge to that of other disciplines both inside and outside the school setting. See Figure 7.7

Figure 7.7. Questions about Connections

Do the materials include	Text X	Text Y	Text Z
☐ Opportunities to use (or discover more about) other subject areas: math, science, history, geography, art, literature, music, health, and others?			
☐ Opportunities to build upon prior experiences or existing knowledge?			
☐ Methods (graphic organizers and other) that enable students to clearly see these connections to other disciplines?			
☐ Themes to facilitate interdisciplinary projects?			
☐ Projects that require learners to use technology, print or visual media and/or personal interviews to acquire information?			
TOTALS			

Standard 4: Comparisons

Locate sections that compare the foreign language to English. See Figure 7.8.

Figure 7.8. Questions about Language Comparisons

Are students asked	Text X	Text Y	Text Z
☐ To look at their own language and compare it linguistically to the target language?			
☐ To investigate or discuss cognates, idioms, and "borrowed words" in both English and the target language?			
TOTAL			

Locate activities in the book where students can compare their own culture to that of speakers of the foreign language. See Figure 7.9.

Figure 7.9. Questions about Cultural Comparisons

Ask	Text X	Text Y	Text Z
☐ Are students asked to compare and/or contrast their own culture with the target culture to discover similarities and differences?			
☐ Do the activities invite students to explore aspects of their own culture further (surveys, research, etc.)?			
☐ Does the text present similarities as well as differences in cultures?			
☐ Does the text allow students to demonstrate knowledge of the difference(s) between their culture and that of target language speakers?			
TOTALS			

Standard 5: Communities

Locate areas and activities in the text and ancillaries that suggest using the language beyond the classroom. See Figure 7.10.

Figure 7.10. Questions about Community

Does the text	Text X	Text Y	Text Z
☐ Encourage/ask students to communicate with foreign language speakers outside the classroom (orally or in writing)?			
☐ Promote projects that use community resources and/or involve interaction with members of the community?			
☐ Identify careers or situations in which proficiency in the target language is useful or required?			
☐ Identify famous people who speak the target language?			
☐ Suggest and encourage participation in opportunities for leisure activities that use the target language (media, sports, games, travel, music, reading)?			
☐ Incorporate technology, for example, suggest engaging, worthwhile Internet activities?			
TOTALS			

Totaling the Scores

I encourage anyone thinking about using these charts to have some open, meaningful discussion in your department (or with yourself) and to personalize this evaluation instrument. Eliminate any of the aspects of it that do not fit:

♦ Your instructional goal(s)

♦ Your teaching situation (class size, traveling teacher, etc.)

♦ Your schedule configuration (length of class, not offered daily, etc.)

♦ Your teaching style

There are several ways to draw a conclusion from the question charts. One is to simply add the number of points in each section for each text, and see which text got the most. However, because some sections have many more points possible, you might conceivably choose a text that is very Standard 1 (Communication)–centered, but neglects a couple other goals. To avoid this, I'd suggest using one the grids shown in Figures 7.11 and 7.12.

Figure 7.11. Text Selection Grid

Standard	Best text	Middle text	Least
1: Communication			
2: Cultures			
3: Connections			
4: Comparisons			
5: Communities			

To use the grid in Figure 7.11, look at each section, and see which of the three texts evaluated was Best, Least, or the one that fell in the Middle. Write the text name (or letter) in the grid, and it should quickly become obvious which does the best overall job in the most categories, by reading downward under each text.

The alternate table in Figure 7.12 reverses the categories.

Figure 7.12. Alternate Text Selection Grid

Standards	1: Communication	2: Cultures	3: Connections	4: Comparisons	5: Communities
Text X					
Text Y					
Text Z					

In the table in Figure 7.12, each text would be rated either 1 (Best), 2 (Middle) or 3 (Least) for each category, and the text that is superior in the most categories would be quickly visible.

Bibliography

General References

Covey, Steven R. *The 7 Habits of Highly Effective People.* New York: Simon and Schuster Inc.,1990.

Curtain, Helena A., and Pesola, Carol A. *Languages and Children—Making the Match: Foreign Language Instruction in the Elementary School.* Reading, MA: Addison-Wesley Publishing Company, Inc., 1988.

Standards for Foreign Language Learning in the 21st Century. Yonkers, NY: National Standards in Foreign Language Education Collaborative Project, 1999.

Suggested Teacher Resources

♦ The best, bar none, if you have a question, is FLTEACH. Find the archives as well as subscription information on the Internet at http://listserv.buffalo.edu/archives/flteach.html. On any given day, more than 2,000 foreign language teachers read whatever is posted, and give advice and helpful information. "Picking brains" is encouraged, and usually fruitful.

♦ In addition to the National Standards, the ACTFL released listening standards in 1998, speaking standards in 1999, and writing standards in 2002. These are useful in evaluating your students' performances. Here are their Internet addresses:

- Listening http://www.sil.org/lingualinks/languagelearning/otherresources/actflproficiencyguidelines/ACTFLGuidelinesListening.htm

- Speaking http://www.sil.org/lingualinks/languagelearning/otherresources/actflproficiencyguidelines/ACTFLGuidelinesSpeaking.htm

- Writing http://www.sil.org/lingualinks/languagelearning/OtherResources/ACTFLProficiencyGuidelines/ACTFLGuidelinesWriting.htm

Technology: The Big Three

♦ Trackstar: A free site for creating web searches (or modifying/using those already there) is at http://trackstar.hprtec.org. (Note: Do not type www into this address; it won't work.)

♦ Blue Web'n is at http://www.kn.pacbell.com/wired/bluewebn. Here you can find over 1000 outstanding Internet learning sites categorized by subject area, audience, and type (lessons, activities, projects, resources, references, and tools).

♦ About.com has immense resources for French, Spanish, German, and Latin. Find the foreign languages section at http://7-12educators.about.com/cs/foreignlanguages/index.htm.